Stand Up and Garden

MARY MOSS-SPRAGUE

THE COUNTRYMAN PRESS
WOODSTOCK, VT

Photographs by the author unless otherwise specified
Book design and composition by Faith Hague

Published by The Countryman Press, P.O. Box 748,
Woodstock, VT 05091
Distributed by W. W. Norton & Company, Inc.,
500 Fifth Avenue, New York, NY 10110
Printed in the United States of America

10 9 8 7 6 5 4 3 2 1

Stand Up and Garden
978-0-88150-983-0

The glossary of terms at the end of chapter 7 and editorial assistance
for that section was kindly supplied by Dripworksusa.com. The author
gratefully acknowledges their assistance.

635

To my late mother,
Ruby Ruth Fitzgerald Mackie,
my first gardening teacher and inspiration.
Her aching back would have loved
these off-the-ground methods!

Contents

Acknowledgments

Many thanks to Greg Aspinall, for his terrific skill with the camera; Dud and Nan Carlson, for their help with photographs and for being my best "students" in learning and improving upon these aboveground gardening methods; Agnes Dickens (Nan's mother), for gamely navigating the garden for a photo shoot; Oregon State University Cooperative Extension Service and Cornell University Cooperative Extension Service, Wayne County, and especially Laurie VanNostrand, for all of the great master gardener training and teaching opportunities I received from CCE here in upstate New York; my talented daughter, Kathren Moss, for her dedication and talent in creating all of this book's wonderful illustrations; and finally, my beloved and long-suffering husband, Albert Clark Sprague, who willingly helped all he could in the gardening tasks and cheered me on during the effort involved in writing this book.

The author (left) chats with Dud and Nan Carlson.   GREG ASPINALL

Introduction

Does kneeling on the ground to grow plants send you scrambling for aspirin? Do you dread the idea of bending and crouching to plant seeds, set out transplants, and keep the garden weeded? All of the necessary digging, tilling, picking out rocks, and trying to achieve a level area is a real hassle and hard on the body. Sure, it's good exercise, but maybe you'd prefer to save your leisure exercise time and effort for something more fun. *I* sure would!

Having inherited my sainted mother's osteoarthritis, I discovered many years ago that in-ground gardening just wasn't working for me. The price I paid for putting in hours of the painful work involved was just too much. Fortunately, before I gave up on the whole process of growing my own herbs and vegetables, a neighbor friend turned me on to the concept of gardening with straw-based raised beds. This method is just perfect for all kinds of herbs, radishes, scallions, and smaller plants, and, in chapter 5, you'll see how this revolutionary technique will give you a whole new approach to gardening.

Eventually, I was able to enroll in and graduate from the master gardener course offered by the extension service in my state. This helped me become a much better gardener at home while I helped others solve their own gardening problems.

A couple of years later, the ground in my usual tomato planting area was found to be rife with verticillium wilt. Nearly all of my newly planted, healthy tomato plants bit the dust from this fungal disease. Not being one to accept adversity without fighting back, I got the inspiration to lay out Typar, a nifty weed barrier

The trellises fill up quickly with plants going upward.   GREG ASPINALL

material, and set out another batch of tomato plants, all in containers, on it. I followed that by installing a micro-drip irrigation system for the plants, which made keeping everybody watered properly a snap.

Everybody was happy then: me, the plants, and all of those who enjoyed the resulting bountiful tomato harvest. At that point, I was totally converted to growing everything up off the ground, and I've never looked back. I could—and do—literally "stand up and garden."

People are now getting into what is often described as "vertical gardening," and their techniques can be used to great advantage. You'll find that many people have great ideas of their own and are constantly innovating new stuff. See chapter 11 for good ideas from other people that I've come across over the past couple of years.

Hundreds of visitors to my garden used to ask me, "Where can I find the book that shows how to do all this stuff, especially the straw-bale raised bed?" I finally realized that I'd better write that book, because no one else has done it.

So here it is: a book containing all of the instructions, supply lists, and explanations of what you need to know in order to have a successful, prolific, off-the-ground garden. I've even included a chapter on composting, as well as everything you'll need to know about laying out a micro-drip irrigation system. I figure that using one comprehensive book beats the heck out of confusedly flipping through five different volumes in order to find the necessary information.

Enjoy yourself as you discover how you can stand up and garden!

1
Thinking Differently About Vegetable Gardening

PLENTY OF PEOPLE are beginning to embrace "vertical gardening" methods, and for good reason. If you've never thought of—or known about—gardening aboveground, then this book will be an eye-opener for you. You'll learn how to grow vegetables and herbs with innovative techniques and without the kneeling, tilling, digging, weeding, and other hassles.

This book differs from others on this topic because it shows and explains techniques not included in them. It will guide you into a new, "all-gain, no-pain" style of gardening that will make you a convert. You'll wonder why on earth you ever went through the hassles of growing plants in the ground when this way is so much easier!

You'll learn how to make a waist-high, raised growing bed using straw as a base, simple trellises requiring no nails or screws

Figure 1.1 It's easy to maintain your garden when there's no kneeling involved!   GREG ASPINALL

that can be constructed in about 30 minutes, a nifty drip irrigation system, custom soil mixes, and a system for making your own compost. Along the way, you'll also learn how to deal with plant diseases, garden pests, and other hot topics that will help you succeed in your gardening efforts.

Will I have to buy a lot of expensive or clunky new tools? you ask. The amount of "stuff" you'll need for aboveground gardening is pretty modest and will be described within each topical chapter, including actual supply lists for specific projects. If you've ever had a garden before, you may very well already have most of the necessary tools. The only exception may be in the items needed to build the straw-bale garden box. After looking over the supply list for that project (see chapter 5), though, you'll probably find that it won't be that difficult to round up the few necessary tools.

It may be that you already enjoy gardening. It's certainly good exercise and gets you out in contact with nature. Perhaps the process of getting your hands into the soil, planting seeds, and reaping the tasty harvest as summer progresses into fall gives you immense personal satisfaction. Maybe your family had a vegetable garden when you were young, and you've been thinking you'd like to return to those days, but you're just plain turned off now by the prospect of the backbreaking work involved.

Or perhaps you're strongly motivated to grow your own veggies and herbs because of concerns about food safety. That makes sense; numerous national and international incidents of nasty E. coli and other bacteria- and toxin-based food-borne illness have brought this topic to front and center. Most food scares in recent years have resulted from human error in processing and handling produce, including contamination from poor sanitation

Figure 1.2. Harvesting for supper in your own backyard can bring peace of mind.   GREG ASPINALL

practices, chemicals, and other substances. Knowing exactly where your fresh food comes from—vegetables in particular—creates peace of mind, with better health resulting from safe food consumption.

What about weeds? you mutter, your scalp prickling in anticipation of what you think is an inevitable endless cycle of pulling and digging. Mention weeds, and most people shudder. Well, what about them? The chore of keeping an in-ground garden weeded becomes a moot point if you stand up and garden. There just won't be any weed issues. Wouldn't that make your day?

> **The chore of keeping an in-ground garden weeded becomes a moot point if you stand up and garden.**

When putting in a traditional in-ground garden, fossil fuel consumption also comes into play if gas-powered machines, such as tractor plows and rototillers, are used. High gas prices are discouraging, and one doesn't want to waste precious resources. Using the methods described within this book will put those concerns into the category of "does not apply."

Oh, yeah, and what about all the hassles of watering a garden? Look no further: In chapter 7, I will show you exactly how to set up a very flexible, micro-drip irrigation system. (Also, a list of suppliers is included.) When water is directed only to the root zones of vegetables, the amount of water required (and used) to sustain plants diminishes dramatically. And when installed with a timer, this system will automatically provide the correct amount of water needed for each plant with no waste or mess. If your gardening space is some distance away—even 100 feet or more—from a water source, not to worry! Micro-drip irrigation works very well with a long-distance watering situation. Multiple hoses can handily be linked together and stretched out a good distance from water faucets.

There's no point in growing things that don't fit in your diet, so think about what you (and other members of your household, if you have them) like to eat. Do crunchy fresh cucumbers and flavorful string beans make your mouth water? Does the thought of roasted summer squash or stir-fried sugar snap peas get your tummy rumbling with anticipation? Many people love fresh cherry tomatoes and also pickle or can them for a treat during the winter. Growing and pickling cucumbers along with your own fresh dill and giving jars of them as holiday gifts can be a very satisfying experience. There are endless possibilities when it comes to fresh vegetables and herbs.

However, what will grow well where you live? For regions with a regular, warm growing season—and regions with warm to moderate climates year-round—the sky's the limit. Tomatoes, pep-

Figure 1.3. Nature's bounty: All were harvested from a vertical garden.
GREG ASPINALL

pers, eggplant, beans, lettuces and various greens, peas, turnips, beets, leeks, parsnips, cauliflower, broccoli, rutabagas, squash, radishes, celery, all kinds of herbs, carrots, potatoes, cucumbers, melons, pumpkins, and more—with all of their delightful varieties—can grow beautifully in containers, on trellises, or in the special, 3-foot-high raised beds sized perfectly for the need. (The one exception is corn. Trying to grow corn in raised beds or containers isn't likely to be successful. It is the one vegetable that I'll buy from local farmer's markets while it is in season, and I dry or can whatever isn't eaten while it's fresh on the cob. If you want to till up an area for planting corn, though, certainly do so. It's your garden!)

By using the aboveground gardening methods explained in this book, you can easily grow both cold-season crops and warm-

Figure 1.4. A new head of cauliflower displays its beauty.   GREG ASPINALL

season crops (unless you live in an extreme climate). Lettuce, peas, and most of the cabbage and onion families grow best in spring and fall, when the weather is cool. Most can survive a light frost. Check with your state's extension service or a good annual farmer's almanac for precise growing information for your particular geographical/climate region. (In fact, I always unabashedly recommend that new gardeners, particularly, establish contact with their state's cooperative extension service office. Each state/county extension office has trained agents and maintains extensive libraries with prepared handouts of helpful literature and how-to information. They have websites, too, for those who find it more convenient to look for substantiated, reliable enlightenment on the Internet. That way, if you have questions not answered by this book, you have a ready source of answers.)

The yields of produce you'll grow will make you a believer. Instead of sickly or stunted plants that must be pulled out of the ground and tossed, you'll have wonderfully healthy plants heavily laden with yummy vegetables. And wait until you see what happens to herbs when they're grown up off the ground—they love it! They'll bush out and grow prolifically.

Now that you've thought about what vegetables you will grow, where will you plant them? The site of your vegetable garden should be in solid sunshine for most of the day, receiving no fewer than six hours of *direct* sunlight daily. If the ground isn't relatively level, don't be discouraged. Highly individual, creative approaches can be used to set out containers and straw-bale gardens, and even special trellises, to grow crops on uneven ground. (Note: The trellis design shown in chapter 4 isn't going to be the best for a hillside or other uneven terrain. A terraced style would be better for such a situation.)

Brainstorming is a great idea. Make a map of your gardening area to help you visualize its appearance and make the best use of space. Whether you have a large yard, a spacious patio, or a tiny

Figure 1.5. A bed full of herbs—rosemary, oregano, basils   GREG ASPINALL

backyard, you can grow plenty of food by using the right layout and methods. Even a deck of any size can be used to grow plants in containers of various sorts.

As you assess your gardening space on your property, keep in mind that you should never place containers, trellises, or raised beds directly below or very close to trees. Why? While trees provide all kinds of environmental benefits, they can shade your crops and create uneven moisture problems because of rain and shade issues.

For optimum success, do choose a growing site that's protected from high winds. Other considerations, such as having good air circulation for disease prevention and avoiding low-lying frost pockets, are important as well. This really isn't rocket science, just common sense.

Are you convinced and pumped up, ready to go? Oops—hold on! Before you charge into your designated gardening space and start building the trellises and other structures shown in this book, browse through the pertinent chapters. Doing so will help you start to form your own direction and make the decisions necessary to ensure your gardening success. And, as mentioned earlier, you'll spot photographs, drawings, and necessary supply lists, so you'll be able to round up everything you need prior to undertaking this new venture. Your shopping list shouldn't break the bank, however. Whether you choose to grow all of your plants from seed or purchase them elsewhere, you can enjoy all of nature's bounty produced from within a compact space and with a minimum of expense.

In fact, these gardening techniques encourage thriftiness and frugality! In this book, you'll discover how one-dollar plastic dishpans serve as ideal containers from which numerous vining plants will launch themselves forth to climb up a trellis. Old bathtubs, livestock watering troughs, and washtubs work beautifully for growing root vegetables, including potatoes. Larger 3- to 5-gallon

grower's pots or other large containers will accommodate carrots, beets, and other deep-root vegetables, and anything else you wish to grow.

And the economy doesn't stop there. Also think of the possibilities when you can easily spread out or stagger plantings of certain vegetables. Trying to do so with an in-ground garden is a huge hassle. Unless you religiously hoe and refertilize the soil and replant certain determinate-growth crops every few weeks, you wind up with all of the lettuce, radishes, beans, or peas, for instance, ready for harvest all at once. With containers, trellises, and straw-bale box gardens, you can easily replant a little bit every week or two, rotating and harvesting crops over an extended period. This obviously extends the growing season, giving you more opportunity to enjoy the garden goodies.

> **Plants growing up off the ground aren't as easy prey for hungry, creepy-crawly critters.**

Finally, what about pests and disease? Plants growing up off the ground aren't as easy prey for hungry, creepy-crawly critters. Slugs, too, can be easily spotted and dealt with should they dare to climb up for a bite. And with plants growing in containers, removing and isolating a diseased or otherwise troubled plant can be done in a jiffy before it contaminates the others. (This subject is covered in chapter 10.)

Okay, you've been reading this and thinking, that's all well and good but, doggone it, at my apartment or home, I don't even have a deck, balcony, porch, or postage-stamp-sized yard for a garden! There just isn't *any* usable space for growing vegetables. Now what?

Well, how about a friend's backyard (sharing the space), a rooftop garden, or a community garden? The aboveground gardening methods and techniques demonstrated in this book can be and are being easily adapted for use anywhere. Towns and cities frequently allocate vacant lots for community gardens. Residents in numerous towns and cities across the nation, including bigger cities like Seattle, New York, Portland, and Los Angeles, are already gardening in unused plots of public land donated by local governments and in sections of privately owned land with the owner's permission. Go online or check with your local extension service to find locations already being used for community gardens.

Or why not start a community garden yourself? A little research will lead you to other like-minded individuals and groups who share your gardening vision. Share with them the ideas from this book. You just might inspire more people to get into the project.

By now I hope you are heartened by the possibilities of finally being able to grow all of the vegetables and herbs you want without any of the usual hassle. With that thought in mind, let's get your garden off the ground!

2 Using Weed Barrier

I STRONGLY RECOMMEND that you place weed barrier under the designated space for your containers, underneath the straw-bale garden space, and on the space that will hold your trellis. And this chapter will tell you everything you need to know about using a weed barrier.

Wait, hold on here! *Why*, you ask, should I use weed barrier, and what the heck is it, anyway?

A weed barrier consists of a layer of some material—even newspapers—laid on top of the ground to prevent the growth and proliferation of weeds. This makes for a much cleaner, weed-free growing area and pays for itself in one season. Sure, you could choose to use a chemical weed killer, but "better living through chemistry" is not necessarily a motto to be followed where our Earth is involved. Weed killer chemicals are nasty, dangerous, and cause all kinds of problems to all living things unless they're applied with scrupulous care. Also, they usually contaminate water

runoff, which leads to more problems down the line. That is why using a weed barrier works out better all around.

Newspapers are available from a variety of public sources. While they can be used in a pinch (or by penny-pinching necessity!), I strongly recommend using either a landscape fabric weed barrier or Typar weed barrier instead. These can be purchased by the roll in most home and garden supply centers. They are great for gardens since they prevent weeds from popping up while allowing moisture to pass through.

You won't believe how clean and orderly your vegetable garden area will be.

If you want to get something even stronger and longer lasting, check with agricultural supply stores. They will know about—and possibly sell—a very nice, strong material used by many garden centers, commercial nurseries, and other agribusinesses. It's heavier and more durable than the kinds commonly available for the average consumer, and it also still allows water to filter through. There are a couple of manufacturer names to look for: Marafi landscape fabric and De-Witt Weed Barrier. The latter offers 15- and 20-year rated woven polypropylene fabric that is excellent for landscape use.

Weed barrier is especially ideal for the gardening techniques described in this book, and it is helpful when installing a drip irrigation system (see chapter 7), which can be laid out neatly and cleanly on the covered ground surface when soil and weeds underfoot aren't present, trying to complicate things and make a mess. Also, if your vegetable garden is adjacent to a lawn, having a clean line of weed barrier makes mowing right up to the edge of the area so much neater and easier. (See fig. 2.1.) You won't believe how clean and orderly your vegetable garden area will be.

The looser the weave of weed barrier, such as the fabric/cloth

Figure 2.1. Dishpans and grower's pots, all full of plants and kept neatly on the weed barrier. GREG ASPINALL

kind, the more chance there is of weeds sneaking up through any slight tears or other openings. Putting down a thick layer of newspaper first will make that less likely. However, the Typar barrier, which is a smooth, plastic composite (not the same as black plastic!), works better and lasts much longer. Using it will not require putting newspaper down first. As the manufacturer directly states, "It is strong enough to block weeds yet porous enough to ensure the passage of necessary water in your planter areas and around trees. This product is produced from 20%–33% post-industrial recycled materials."

Designating the Space for Your Weed Barrier

The first step in laying down any kind of weed barrier is to determine the space where it will be needed. This involves measuring

and marking off the area that you will be using for your containers, raised bed, and trellis. Grouping all three types of growing methods into a compact area is ideal and saves a lot of walking around in the process. It's the most efficient layout for drip irrigation and will also be necessary if you have a compact or restricted space available for your gardening endeavors. Remember that you will need sufficient space between rows of containers to allow for expansion of the plants and installation of tubing, emitters, and sprayers if you choose to use micro-drip irrigation, as well as walking space around the straw-bale garden box, access to the trellis from all sides, and just general maneuvering room.

Be sure to consider the dimensions of the area to be covered when you purchase the weed barrier. Most weed barrier materials come in 24- to 48-inch-wide rolls; the length may be anywhere from 25 to 1,000 feet. I prefer to always have some on hand, because extending a garden area is often a possibility. Also, it comes in handy for various gardening projects; you just never know when you might need to put some down.

No matter which weed barrier method you choose, if you are constructing one or more of the straw-bale raised beds (chapter 5), lay the weed barrier down first. If you are building one or more trellises, wait until the construction of them is finished, and then cut and fit the weed barrier underneath, taking care to snug it up around the in-ground supports.

Laying Down the Weed Barrier

Once you have designated your gardening space, it's time to lay down the weed barrier.

Newspaper/Wood Chips

If you aren't going to use commercial weed barrier, you can use the newspaper/wood chip method. This requires:

- a generous supply of old newspapers
- a garden hose with a nozzle that's connected to a water supply
- a substantial supply of wood chips

Open the newspapers and begin laying them on the ground so that they cover and overlap all of the surface where you want to prevent weeds. Layer them on at least three pages thick; you can use more depending on your newspaper supply. Then spray them with water from the hose. Don't soak them thoroughly; just spray enough water to keep them from blowing around while you work. Dump out and spread the wood chips in a layer on top of the newspapers. Make it a thick layer of at least 2 to 3 inches; you shouldn't be able to see any of the newspapers when you're done.

The newspapers will eventually decompose enough to allow weeds to sneak up from or down into the soil.

Bear in mind that the newspapers will eventually decompose enough to allow weeds to sneak up from or down into the soil. At that point, you'll have to keep putting more newspaper down, which means clearing off the wood chips first, wetting down the paper, and then redistributing the wood chips. After repeating this process again and again, you might just decide that it's worth it to purchase either the fabric or Typar barrier (both referred to hereafter as commercial weed barrier).

Commercial Weed Barrier

If you're using commercial weed barrier, forget the newspapers and collect the following:

- commercial weed barrier
- a pair of scissors
- some U-shaped wire garden staples (in general, for a piece of barrier that is 36 inches × 60 inches, you'll require about 16 to 18 staples, each placed approximately 12 inches apart)
- a hammer

You can install the barrier directly on top of the ground. It doesn't matter if it's on top of grass or soil; it works well on either surface. Be sure to remove any existing wrapping from the roll of barrier material first.

One person can do this, but it's much easier if you have a helper. One person should stand at one end of the designated area, holding the roll, while the second person pulls on the cut

Figure 2.2. Plants are filling up space in the straw bale gardens, with containerized tomato plants lurking nearby.

end while walking along to the other end of the designated bound-
ary. However, if you're limited to doing this alone, simply pull
some of the fabric from the roll to get it started, place a brick or
heavy stone on that end, and then lay the roll on the ground and
pull on it to unroll it the length of the desired area.

When the first length of the commercial weed barrier is in
place, cut off that length from the roll and, starting at one end of
the material, place the pointy ends of one of the U-shaped wire
staples onto the fabric. Use the hammer to gently pound it into
the ground through the material, just as if you're hammering a
nail or staple into wood. (See fig. 2.3.) The result should be that
you see just the horizontal top bar of the staple holding down the

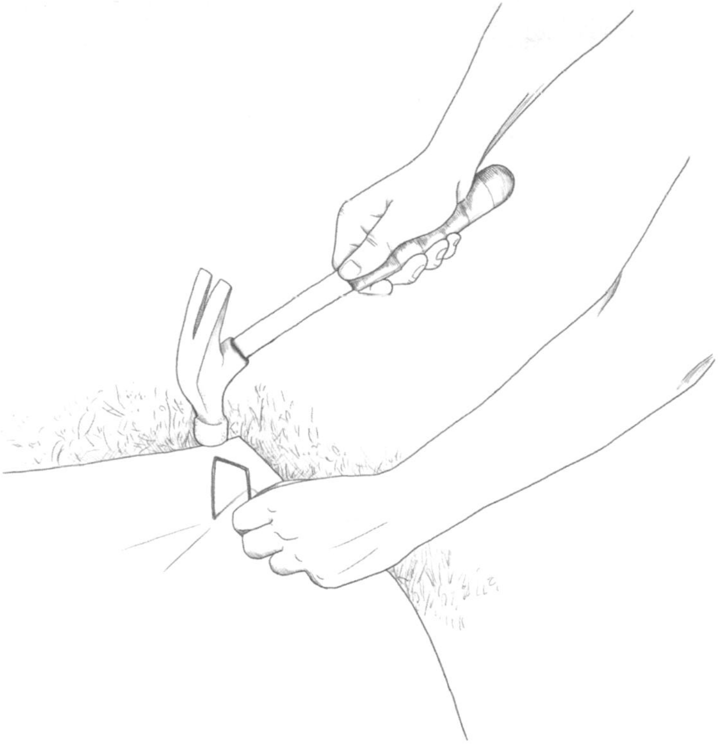

Figure 2.3

Figure 2.4. Here's a look at the garden area, complete with greenhouse in background.

barrier material. If your material is 24 to 30 inches wide, put in at least three staples across the width of the end. Then go over to the other end, pull the material tight, and put at least three staples across the end. Repeat this process with the barrier material, stapling down the length and making sure to overlap at least an inch along the place where the edges of each strip meet. Then place staples all along that seam at 12-inch intervals to connect the two pieces and fasten them down securely. The end result should look similar to a carpeted floor.

To avoid snagging woven fabric and creating holes, and to avoid slipping or falling on the barrier material, cover the whole area with a generous, 1-inch-thick layer of wood chips, bark dust, or mulch. You can also use pea gravel, although it costs more, but

I strongly recommend the wood chips. Sure, a stray weed seed can occasionally land on wood chips or bark dust and try to establish itself, but there's no soil for it to root into, so you can quickly pull it out.

Now you can build your straw-bale garden(s) and set up your trellis(es). When your containerized plants or seedlings are ready, set them out on the barrier-covered area and, if applicable, lay out the drip irrigation system (see chapter 7). See figure 2.4 for an example of a finished area, with a straw-bale garden, containers with plants, and a trellis.

3 Containers— Your Chance to Get Creative on the Cheap!

SHOULD YOU BE BRAND NEW to the gardening scene, be assured that there is no one shape of container that's more "correct" for garden use than another. Long, short, wide, square, round— all are perfectly good. This also applies to materials from which the containers are made. Wood, ceramic, pottery, fiberglass, plastic/resin/polyethylene—it's wide open to personal choice and economical considerations. If you already have a container collection, make certain that it is suited to the plants you want to grow before you charge gung-ho into planting. Reading the rest of this chapter will help you decide if you need anything different. Remember one very important thing: Your containers *must* all have drainage holes or be able to withstand having holes drilled in them without breaking apart. Without proper drainage, your plants are doomed to fail.

Certainly, there are many very attractive (and expensive) pots and planters available in stores. The more utilitarian choices usually cost far less. Containers can often be found at yard sales, thrift stores, and other secondhand vendors, and I encourage you to go scouting for what you need before buying anything. Five-gallon food-grade service buckets can often be had for free at supermarkets or restaurants. Whiskey barrels cut in half work well; even large old truck tires will serve, when placed flat on the ground and the hollow filled with soil, although they're not very aesthetically pleasing. Plant nurseries and garden centers sometimes sell off unneeded inventory, too, and you may be able to find some great containers at these places.

This is especially true if you're in the market for larger, molded plastic tubs, also known as grower's pots. If you don't find these big fellas locally, the Internet is a great place to buy them at inexpensive prices. Just set your search engine for something like "plastic grower's pots," and you should find plenty of vendors who will be happy to ship to you. Three-, 4-, and 5-gallon pots can cost as little as a dollar apiece, maybe even less. The only catch is that there is usually a minimum order of 50 or 100. But that shouldn't be a problem if you have friends or relatives who also want these containers. Simply share the cost of a shipment, and you're in business!

Here's an innovative idea: One of the thriftiest choices I've found are thick, black, rectangular polyethylene dishpans sold in dollar stores for—yes!—just one dollar. Thin, brittle plastic pans won't work, though; the material must be a bit resilient and flexible. Polyethylene is the same material used for making livestock watering tubs, so it's safe for this application.

Take a look at figure 3.1 to see what some of the choices are and decide what you want. Then start looking.

While the shape of containers and the material they're made of aren't important, we do need containers of different sizes. But

Figure 3.1. Food-grade buckets, grower's pots, and plastic dishpans are all good for growing plants, just remember to add drainholes.

why? It's necessary because it's not a one-size-fits-all world. A thriving Roma or beefsteak tomato plant bearing heavy fruit must reside in a container that can withstand the plant's weight and bulk, such as a 5-gallon grower's pot or food-grade bucket. This container must also be large and deep enough for heavy wire or wooden support stakes that will be added as the plant grows. All plants requiring soil 6 or more inches deep belong in the largest grower's pots. (See fig. 11.9 in chapter 11, which illustrates 5-gallon food-grade buckets being used in the garden.)

Of course, if you have or can find animal watering tubs or troughs that can have holes drilled in them, they also make excellent planters. They can even be cut down if either the top or bottom has been crushed or cracked. Old bathtubs already have a drain, so they, too, can be used. All of these are ideal for root vegetables, including potatoes, beets, parsnips, carrots, and so on. Tubs and troughs can also be used in conjunction with a vertical

Figure 3.2. Al Sprague drills holes in several plastic dishpans at a time.

GREG ASPINALL

trellis, which means that beans, peas, and other climbers could call them home.

Let's say that you've found the black polyethylene dishpans—what to do now? Drill five holes in the bottom of each dishpan, one in each corner and one in the center (see fig. 3.2). Fill the pan with soil and put in the seeds, inserting and covering them as directed on the seed packets. Then watch them climb up onto trellises: Peas, beans, squash, pumpkins, cucumbers, cherry tomatoes, large sweet and chili peppers, and other edibles are perfectly happy getting their starts in these pans. And they will oblige nicely by clinging to trellis netting as they make their way up toward the sun. (See fig. 3.3.) With a ground weed barrier already

Figure 3.3. Beans and peas planted directly in the dishpans quickly germinate and start climbing. GREG ASPINALL

in place, there will be no weeds to deal with, and watering these containers appropriately is easy. It's really child's play, of course, if you install a micro-drip irrigation system.

As noted earlier, most noncherry varieties of tomatoes need the solidity, depth, and breadth of a large container. If beets, turnips, rutabagas, Brussels sprouts, parsnips, celery, leeks, spinach, carrots, eggplant, Swiss chard, cauliflower, broccoli, cabbages, and other large or root vegetables are on your "must" list, they, too, should be planted in the big, deep pots. On the other hand, a smaller pot can easily accommodate herb plants such as parsley and basil, as long as you plan to keep the plant well trimmed at a size that can be managed. The smaller 2- and 3-gallon pots are generally fine for other easily contained herbs, salad greens, scallions, shallots, radishes, smaller chili peppers that aren't destined for a trellis, and so forth. For growing strawberries, however, I recommend the straw-based raised bed (chapter 5).

> I suggest you err on the side of choosing containers that are too large rather than too small.

Most of the ideas in this book lean toward thrift and saving money. And it all boils down to personal choice; there are no "rights" and "wrongs" when it comes to containers, other than the size, drainage, and depth issues previously mentioned. You must select the ones that are going to work best for you. Some experimentation will help; when in doubt, I suggest you err on the side of choosing containers that are too large rather than too small. Successfully repotting a vegetable plant midseason because it has outgrown its container is virtually impossible due to severe plant shock that will occur when its roots are disturbed.

The last thing to consider when choosing the sizes and shapes of the containers you'll be using is where you're going to set them

Figure 3.4. Swiss chard shows off its pretty leaves. GREG ASPINALL

Figure 3.5. Tomato plants, up close and personal   GREG ASPINALL

out on the weed barrier. How much space do you have for gardening? Will some of them be used for large, individual plants, such as tomatoes? Is there room for one or more trellises? (Skim through chapter 4 to see what's involved.)

If you followed the suggestions laid out in chapter 1, you probably have already scoped out the space situation and know about how much square footage you have for your gardening efforts. Have you sketched it all out on paper to eliminate some of the guesswork? If not, be sure to do that now, before you start building trellises and raised beds, and filling containers with soil!

4 "Growing Up" is Easy with This Trellis

LET'S FACE IT: Very few people truly enjoy the hassle of trying to control wayward vining plants. As cucurbits such as squash, cucumbers, and melons grow, they start wandering all over the place. Ditto with string beans and peas. Cherry tomato plants also need some kind of guidance to keep them under control. That turns weeding, watering, disease control, and harvesting into an all-out battle. Trying to reach through a tangle of pea and bean vines to remove encroaching weeds can result in the accidental removal of the desired vegetable plants. (All of which makes this an excellent place to use weed barrier!)

Another problem encountered with vining plants, particularly squash, cucumbers, and pumpkins, is that they don't like water standing on their leaves. This predisposes them to mold, mildew, and other nasty stuff. When these plants can grow vertically, up

Figure 4.1. Grape tomatoes revel in the sunshine.   GREG ASPINALL

off the ground, water can cascade off their leaves, leaving them dry and happy.

If one is young, ambitious, and up for the challenge, using traditional gardening methods to grow the aforementioned plants is fine. However, it's not so easy for older folks or individuals with physical limitations. The time and effort required to maintain healthy plants growing in the ground is considerable, no matter what age the gardener may be.

Here again is an opportunity to think differently about growing vegetables. Plants sown or transplanted into containers and then placed under a trellis to climb up will reward you with prolific output and be far less susceptible to crawling or chomping pests and diseases.

Figure 4.2. It's easy to access scarlet runner beans when they're grown on a trellis.   GREG ASPINALL

In this chapter, I'm going to show you how to construct a very functional, easily constructed trellis for which you'll need only 2 inch × 2 inch lumber, stout garden twine, scissors, a pencil, a sharp shovel or post-hole digger, measuring tape, a cupful of flour or gypsum powder, a stepladder, and a mallet or large rock. There'll be no hammering, using screwdrivers, or fussing with other hardware! And, yes, this will be the *only* digging necessary for this off-the-ground gardening method. You'll not need the shovel again! So you get the idea—this is going to be quick and simple.

Preconstruction Preparation

Let's start at the beginning. First and most importantly, decide what trellis-loving crops you want to grow. Do you enjoy eating cucumbers, summer squash, and cantaloupe? Would you like to grow enough cucumbers to make pickles to be enjoyed long after summer ends? How about snap peas and string beans? Many peo-

Fig. 4.3 Tendrils of a garden pea plant quickly head toward the sun.
CHMEE2/ WIKIMEDIA COMMONS

Figure 4.4. A basket neatly packed with fresh herbs, with lettuce growing down below.   GREG ASPINALL

ple love cherry tomatoes and want to pickle or can them for later use. Growing and harvesting larger crops of these goodies is made far easier with a trellis—or several trellises. So be thinking about what you'll use the trellis for.

Remember, too, that you won't be digging or tilling up the ground over which your trellis will be placed. Instead, you'll be either sowing seeds or transplanting seeding plants directly into the containers in which they'll grow and climb up that trellis. As I said, you'll only need to use a shovel for a few minutes to dig the footing holes.

The trellis in figure 4.4 is 8 feet long and about 8½ feet high. Six 2 inch × 2 inch × 10 foot lengths of lumber form the vertical supports, and seven 2 inch × 2 inch × 8 foot lengths form the crossbars. This basic design can be shortened or lengthened by either increasing or decreasing the lengths of the crossbars and vertical supports. There should be a 2-foot difference in the two: An 8-foot-long trellis uses 10-foot vertical supports; a 6-foot-long trellis needs 8-foot supports.

Before constructing this trellis, scout out location possibilities. The best spot for this particular trellis is on a level, flat spot that receives direct sunlight for most—if not all—of the day. Bear in mind that once the trellis is put into place and completed, you'll be covering that area with weed-barrier fabric. Who needs grass and weeds to grow up around the containers and waste space on the trellis, when using weed barrier (discussed in chapter 2) will prevent it?

Building the Trellis

So let's get started. A helper to lend a second pair of hands isn't essential, but it sure makes this easier.

To construct an 8-foot-long trellis, you'll need the following supplies:

- 6 each 2 inch × 2 inch × 10 foot lumber (the 10-foot length is my standard size, but if you want to scale back the height of the trellis, you'll need shorter lengths)
- 7 each 2 inch × 2 inch × 8 foot lumber
- 2 balls stout garden twine
- Scissors
- Measuring tape
- Pencil or felt marker
- Mallet or large rock
- 1 cup flour or gypsum powder, or colored spray paint
- Shovel
- Stepladder or safe, high stool (unless you're really, really tall!)

Measure the ground space for the trellis, both length and width, using dots of flour or gypsum powder to mark the four corners. For the 8-foot-long trellis, it's best to place a third set of vertical supports midway between the end supports; that's why the list includes six of these. Make dots for them, too. If you're making a shorter trellis, then two sets of supports will be adequate.

The old carpenter axiom "measure twice, cut once" is a good one to use here. Be sure that you've measured accurately so the support posts will line up squarely and properly. They must face each other and will be crossed at the top, like a tepee support. So make certain

> **The old carpenter axiom "measure twice, cut once" is a good one to use here.**

that the rectangular space for the trellis is aligned straight; otherwise, the supports won't line up, and the whole trellis will be askew. (Note: It is much easier to drive the 10-footers into the

Figure 4.5. These green beans are really doing well as they grow
upwards on the trellis.   FOREST & KIM STARR/ WIKIMEDIA COMMONS

ground if you cut a point on the ground end of the post. Any kind of small saw will work: A handsaw, pruning saw, or a reciprocating saw—such as a sawzall—easily takes care of the job.)

Use a sharp shovel to loosen the soil where the dots are marked, and dig the footing holes 10 to 12 inches deep. Use a mallet or large rock to pound the vertical posts into the ground. At this point, you'll likely be standing on a stepladder or a high, safe stool, unless you're an extra-tall NBA player. As mentioned earlier, cutting a point on the hole-bound post end beforehand helps a great deal but isn't absolutely essential. If the wood isn't pointed, you'll just have to pound a bit harder and longer to drive the post down into the hole.

Okay, let's assume that you've driven the support posts down into the hole about 10 to 12 inches. Now measure and mark a spot 12 inches down from the *top* of each vertical post. Once you're back down on the ground, gently start rocking each pair of posts back and forth from side to side. As you do this, gradually push

Figure 4.6. Cherry tomatoes getting ready to ripen.
SUESKA152/ WIKIMEDIA COMMONS

each set of posts toward each other until they cross at the top like a tepee.

Using the twine, tie each set together a few inches below the crossing point; the twine should go where you marked the 12-inch length from the top of the post. This is where a helper comes in handy to stand on the ground and hold the posts steady; however, it can be done singly if you're up on the ladder all alone.

Repeat this with each set of supports. Then, for best stability, set an 8-foot bar lengthwise in the tepee crossbars and tie it on firmly. Refill the holes with the dirt removed earlier and tamp it down firmly with your feet. Finally, tie the other 8-foot lengths of lumber onto the tepee shapes, horizontally, like ladder steps.

Now it's time to measure and cut some weed barrier to cover the ground beneath the trellis. You can cut it to fit around the upright supports and tack it down firmly with wire ground staples. The newspaper-and-wood-chip method can instead be used here, but if you're not using commercial weed barrier, you'll have to diligently watch out for weeds trying to come up and remove them as soon as you see them.

Using Your Trellis

Hey, now you're ready to use this thing! Place soil-filled containers with bedding plants or seeds directly under the trellis's bottom bars. Slide them halfway under the bottom crossbars so the plants can climb up both the inside and outside of the trellis. (See fig. 4.7.)

You'll probably want to use garden netting, hung on the trellis and fastened with garden ties or twine, to give plants and vines something to grab onto in their upward climb. There are several types of this trellis mesh available commercially; most garden centers and big-box retailers carry them. Or you can use more twine to create your own custom netting or mesh, tailored to the size of the produce that's going to grow up that trellis. Cucumbers, zucchini, cherry tomatoes, small cantaloupes, and other plants will use the trellis; so will pole beans, peas, and other vining plants. Harvesting peas and beans is easier with a medium-sized mesh. You can put it on now or wait until the plants start growing upward; it's your choice. The mesh or netting should hang down to about 3 inches above your dishpans or other containers to give the growing plants something to grab onto.

Some plants will entwine themselves around the supports, while others may need to be tied. You may find enthusiastic cherry tomatoes or other plants actually going up over the top of the trellis; that's okay. Do keep an eye out for vines and tendrils that would appreciate being lifted up over the next closest crossbar.

Figure 4.7. Here are containerized tomato plants, stakes in place, in proximity to squash growing up the trellis.

Figure 4.8. Scarlet runner beans add color going up the trellis.

GREG ASPINALL

When tying up plants, be sure to use ties that will not cut the stems. Commercial ties are available, or you can opt for using stuff you have around the house, such as old pantyhose or soft cloth strips.

> **In sum, trellises save space and make maintenance and harvesting easier.**

Naturally, you can set up micro-drip irrigation to water each of your containers of plants under the trellis (see chapter 7). Or you can water by hand; again, it's your choice. But it sure is simple to run a length of the drip line tubing on the ground down the center of the trellis and then run micro tubing and emitters out to each container. Then the plants get just the right amount of water, and things stay neat beneath the trellis.

In sum, trellises save space and make maintenance and harvesting easier. They also keep the vegetables clean and prevent many some diseases from taking hold. There's not much else to say here except happy harvesting!

5
Gardening with Straw-Based Raised Beds

NOW WE'RE GOING TO GET INTO the really fun stuff. Fasten your seat belts, and let's go!

In chapter 3, you learned that many of the larger vegetables, as well as herbs, can be grown very successfully in containers. For smaller plants or those traditionally grown in rows, there's very good news: You can avoid the in-ground gardening hassles by planting in self-contained, raised beds that use straw as a foundation. This application is especially ideal for nonroot vegetables (although it's beautifully suited for growing radishes), salad greens, herbs, and other small- to medium-sized plants. (By the way, there's no reason why flowers can't be grown in these beds instead of vegetables and herbs. There are endless possibilities for the posies, so keep your mind open and be creative.)

Raised beds, in general, warm up much more quickly than the ground; the straw works to heat things up even faster. This allows

for earlier planting and extends the growing season. Everyone I know who has adopted this way of gardening swears by it, and for good reason, as you'll find out. (This sure beats swearing *at* the garden, doesn't it?)

I will mention that I have seen advertisements for commercially manufactured, portable raised beds that use a kind of scissors mechanism to lower or raise them. Those beds are simply large, shallow boxes or trays that can be filled with soil and are likely best emptied at the end of each growing season and stored inside. They're very expensive, with a price close to a thousand dollars for a unit measuring 5 feet × 8 feet. While they certainly have their place, I think there are better alternatives for people without as much money to spend and/or who are production-oriented gardeners.

Here is your first look at what I'm going to show you how to build (see fig. 5.1). It's my ultimate raised bed! This photo shows the bed (one of three) in position in my garden amid about 65 tomato plants in containers, with trellises (see chapter 4) and the greenhouse in the background.

I first found out about this concept way back in 1996, when I lived in Oregon. My neighbors were very much into growing their own food, and their adult son, Ron, happened to be an Oregon State University Extension Service master gardener (which I was not at the time). When his mother had knee replacement surgery, Ron devised a new way for her to be able to grow vegetables without having to kneel, crouch for an extended period of time, or dig up the ground: a raised bed based on straw bales. When I, already suffering from osteoarthritis, saw the amazing quantities of excellent-quality produce grown by this painless gardening method, I decided that my days of in-ground gardening were over, too! And I loved the way the plants were all raised off the ground, keeping a lot of different pests, weeds, and diseases from attacking them. It just made a lot of sense.

Figure 5.1. Here is a straw-bale raised bed, full of hearty plants, with a trellis behind it and tomato plants in front.

At first, I just imitated what I saw the neighbors doing (isn't that the American way?). I laid six straw bales on the ground in a rectangle, tied them together, and pounded stakes into the ground on the outside edges at the corners and at regular intervals along the bales to hold them together in my chosen configuration. I sprinkled sulfate of ammonia on the bales to keep them from leaching too much nitrogen out of the 8 to 10 inches of good planting soil that I then put on top of the straw.

By then, I was really gung ho and frankly rhapsodizing over the transformation of my garden. In fact, this concept struck me as being so innovative and exciting that I actually called the gardening editor at our state's largest newspaper, based in Portland, and told her about it. She got all excited, too, and showed up almost immediately with a photographer in tow.

Naturally, I gave credit for the concept to my neighbor's son, and the ensuing newspaper article focused on him and how he developed the straw-bale gardening method on his own. On May 10, 1996, the *Oregonian* printed the article, which appeared in the "Living Smart" section. (I appeared with Ron and his mother in the accompanying photo.)

With inspiration comes innovation. While that initial design worked very nicely, I soon realized that there might be a way to contain everything neatly and without allowing the straw to break up too quickly and make a mess. After experimenting with different designs over the years, I have come up with what I consider the ultimate raised bed design, still using straw as a base. However, I've been putting it in loose, rather than keeping it as tied bales. Other people have also come up with similar methods using straw, but few seem to have taken it quite so far as my particular raised-bed box design.

To create your own ultimate raised bed, you'll need to find or buy a *very* large container with good drainage, or just build a big, wood-frame box specifically for this purpose. You'll see how as you move through this chapter. There's no need to get fancy; feel free to use whatever recycled or previously used materials you can find. Or, if you wish, go ahead and splurge on fresh lumber. That way, you know that the box will last a long time.

By the way, the newer pressure-treated lumber is now safe to use for construction that comes into contact with soil containing edible plants. So the old worries about harmful chemicals leaching into the soil no longer apply. If you're still concerned, you can easily line the box with heavy plastic sheeting. It can be easily stapled into place prior to filling the box with straw. However, railroad ties are completely unsafe to use in contact situations with soil and plants, so don't even think about using them for this purpose; they are full of creosote and other dangerous stuff.

Once this box is constructed and filled tightly with straw, and has a thick layer of good soil spread on top, the straw down below heats up and keeps plants on top warm and eager to grow. In fact, the temperature down in the straw tends to stay at about 80°F all the time; I've checked it with a soil thermometer. It's almost like hydroponic gardening, except you're using warm straw instead of water as a heat base.

Tomato plants tend to go crazy in these beds and will take over if you're not careful—don't say I didn't warn you. I tried an experiment wherein I planted one cherry tomato plant in the center of one of these 8 foot × 4 foot beds. It expanded so much that

Figure 5.2. These cherry tomatoes probably won't be on the vine much longer. Yum! JON SULLIVAN/ WIKIMEDIA COMMONS

it took over the whole bed and produced enough cherry tomatoes to feed the whole town (or close to it)!

Herbs, lettuces, peppers, green onions, strawberries, leeks, and other plants absolutely love being kept safely up off the ground, away from pests, weeds, and other hazards. Being so happy, they'll reward you with prolific growth of fine quality produce. If you were to browse through my three big raised beds during a typical growing season, you'd find thriving quantities of romaine, red leaf lettuce, a salad greens blend, cilantro, mint, several varieties of basil, oregano, thyme, radishes of all sorts, two or three different kinds of peppers, parsley, scallions, chives, and red hamburger onions. Spinach also does well in these beds, by the way, although I sometimes plant it in containers. It all depends on what I want to grow in the big raised beds from year to year.

I should add that for those of you living in a more temperate climate, you can grow plants in these raised beds year-round. In Oregon, my basil and other herbs survived well into the cold weather, succumbing only to a heavy frost. For an anticipated lighter frost, I just drape clear plastic sheeting over the box and fasten it down with rocks or bricks. This creates an excellent hotbed and usually staves off frost damage.

> **Vegetables and herbs just don't survive cold temperatures and having 2 feet or more of snow on top of them!**

Now that I live in central upstate New York, I'm stuck with a growing season being distinctly limited by cold winters and lots of snow. Vegetables and herbs just don't survive cold temperatures and having 2 feet or more of snow on top of them! So, depending on your geographical location and local climate, adjust your seasonal planning and expectations accordingly.

Figure 5.3. Basil, as seen here, does well in raised beds.   GREG ASPINALL

Figure 5.4. Harvesting is a snap when you use a raised bed.   GREG ASPINALL

Let's get back to the business at hand. There are so many excellent advantages to using a raised bed as high as this one. The first one is pretty obvious: it's at a comfortable height—3 feet off the ground—and the entire surface is easily reachable from the sides and from the ends. Reaching over at waist height to plant seeds, thin plants, transplant seedlings, and harvest the goodies—all are painless with such a planting bed. Weeding is a snap, because the only ones you'll find growing in these beds are those that blew over in a breeze and decided to take up residence. They're easily seen and quickly removed with one little tug of the hand. No kneeling, no digging, no pain! It's easily fertilized and watered, too, either by hand or by micro-drip irrigation (see chapter 7). Another advantage is that any interlopers such as harmful insects are readily spotted and removed. No pesticides are needed—or wanted.

Actually, your plants will be far less likely to fall victim to ground-crawling bugs and slugs, because hardly any of them will be adventurous enough to make such a high climb. And since they have no idea of what's up on top, there's no visible attraction. You'll find willing allies in various songbirds if you're fortunate enough to have them nearby. I've frequently seen finches, sparrows, and other birds patrolling my bale garden beds and removing anything they think shouldn't be there. Think of it as another twist on IPM (Integrated Pest Management). These feathered friends cling to tall plant stems while their bright little eyes search for lunch on the soil and leaves.

> **There are so many excellent advantages to using a raised bed as high as this one.**

Watch out, beetles and other plant chompers! (Naturally, if you grow strawberries in these boxes, which works great, you'll want

Figure 5.5. This little rascal is keeping an eye on the garden, ready to spot an invading insect.   RICHARD TAYLOR/ WIKIMEDIA COMMONS

to place aviary netting over them, since the fruit will definitely beckon any flying fruit eaters.)

Another big bonus of these beds is that in-ground virus and fungal disease problems, such as verticillium wilt, can't touch tomatoes, potatoes, and other wilt-susceptible plants you might grow in these boxes, because you're using fresh soil from an un-contaminated source (*aren't you?*). Other advantages include excellent drainage; improved soil warming in the spring; a loose, easily aerated layer of soil; controlled row-planting space; and no compaction from foot traffic. Additionally, you won't have feral or domestic cats and dogs using your garden as a poop repository, and children cannot go running through this raised bed as they can in a traditional in-ground planting bed. Toddlers, bless their hearts, cannot reach up high enough to pull out plants, which is always a beguiling temptation with in-ground gardens. (No more "Look what I found, Mommy [or Grandma]!") Rabbits don't jump up that high, either.

About the only wildlife threat this box may attract would be deer. A nice, jaw-level salad bar is hard to resist, but there are methods to discourage Bambi and company from visiting, some of which are discussed in chapter 9. When in doubt, of course, a good fence usually works very well to keep the tall, four-legged munchers out. Our entire garden area is located

> **When in doubt, of course, a good fence usually works very well to keep the tall, four-legged munchers out.**

within the confines of our large dog's outdoor field-wire fenced area. Nothing larger than a cat or chubby rabbit can get in it. Deer could probably jump the fence, but none have ever done so. I expect that the big deterrent is the canine odor; deer don't enjoy tangling with big dogs.

So anyway, how exactly is this big, ultimate raised bed made? The box can be constructed of any size from odd pieces of lumber and chicken wire or hardware cloth you may already have. Having taught classes on this style of gardening for several years, I've seen many variations on my 8 foot × 4 foot × 3 foot box design, and they all work. Again, this is simply a concept and basic design I'm providing; you can tweak it any old way you like. For instance, some folks prefer to use solid 2 inch × 8 inch or 2 inch × 10 inch boards on the sides and ends, and skip the chicken wire or hardware cloth. (See chapter 11 for an example of this.)

See figure 5.6 for what it looks like without the "filling."

The size and design are all a matter of what works best for you and your circumstances. If building a box this large isn't practical, simply scale down the size. An old bathtub, livestock watering

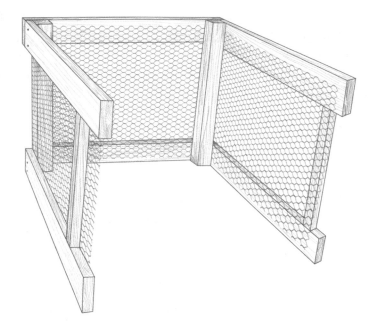

Figure 5.6. This cutaway drawing shows the actual structure of the straw bale raised bed—it's a box!

tub, or any large container with drainage will work, too. Think of it: a garden that's easily planted and weeded, with no kneeling, digging, or other backbreaking discomfort required!

The straw-bale garden shown in figure 5.1 and figure 5.6, heavily constructed for many years of use, is 8 feet long, 4 feet wide, and 3 feet high. Chicken wire stapled around the inside and bottom holds the straw tightly and prevents rodents from tunneling into it. It contains about 12 bales of loose, clean straw, each completely pulled apart and then firmly packed down in the box. (While I stopped using the solid bales several years ago, I just might experiment with it again and use them instead of loose straw in at least one of the beds.)

Ammonium sulfate (or urea) crystals have been sprinkled liberally on the straw and dissolved with water. As mentioned earlier, this prevents nitrogen from leaching out of the soil. At the same time, it also makes the straw break down and start generating heat. Fresh straw was added with each watering and tamped down as firmly as possible to fill the box. This process is described in detail in the "Filling the Box with Straw" section.

When the tightly packed straw is level with the top of the box or other container, as shown in figure 5.7, your favorite planting media can be added. Many commercial planting mixes are available, or a custom mix can be created using peat moss, perlite, good topsoil, sterilized manure, compost, etc. This mix should be placed on top of the straw to a depth of 6 to 8 inches, depending on what you'll be growing in it. Seeds can then be sown directly into the soil, or plant starts can be set in at any stage of development after they've got their second or third set of true leaves. It's best to err on the side of more soil rather than less, in order to

Figure 5.7. Filled with well-packed straw, this raised bed is ready to have soil placed on top.

grow plants with healthy, deep-reaching root systems. Roots with insufficient soil in which to grow downward will remain shallow or even stay on top of the soil, and this spells "failure to thrive" for the life of such plants.

Before building this box on-site (its permanent spot in the garden), I strongly recommend laying down commercial weed barrier that extends quite a bit past the dimensions of the box. (See chapter 2.) This will make for a grass- and weed-free perimeter of the box when it's built. You won't have to be constantly trying to keep the edges around the box free of unwanted green stuff.

Materials List

Lumber

- 1 each 4 inch × 4 inch × 12 foot, pressure treated
- 1 each 2 inch × 4 inch × 8 foot, pressure treated
- 6 each 2 inch × 6 inch × 8 foot, pressure treated

Mesh

- 22½ lineal feet small-hole galvanized chicken wire, 36-inch width (hardware cloth, 1 inch × 2 inch turkey wire, or other strong, galvanized mesh will work)

Hardware

- 32 each ⁵⁄₁₆ inch × 5½ inch galvanized carriage bolts with nuts and washers
- 1 box (1 pound) galvanized staples
- 1 handful 3½-inch galvanized nails

Suggested Tools

- Hammer (always gotta have a hammer!)
- Drill with ⁵⁄₁₆-inch drill bit (needs to drill through 5 inches of wood)
- ½-inch wrench
- Saw (hand or power tool)
- Cutting pliers of some sort
- Tape measure
- Square
- Safety glasses and gloves

Cutting the Box Components

Wear safety glasses and gloves from this point on!

Legs: Measure the 4 inch × 4 inch × 12 foot in half lengthwise. Mark the measurement with the square; cut it there. Measure each cut piece in half, mark that measurement with the square, and make those cuts, yielding four pieces of equal length (about 36 inches).

End rails: Take two of the 2 inch × 6 inch × 8 foot pieces and measure them in half lengthwise, marking with the square. Cut them there, making four pieces of equal length (about 48 inches).

Side rails: The remaining four pieces of 2 inch × 6 inch × 8 foot lumber will be your side rails. They are ready to go as is and don't require any cutting.

Mesh: Cut the wire mesh into two sections 36 inches × 42 inches, and two sections 36 inches × 93 inches. Place one section next to one of the 4 inch × 4 inch legs. The 36-inch width needs to be a little shorter than the leg length so that

it will not stick up above or below the top or bottom rail. If necessary, cut 1 to 2 inches off the 36-inch width so that the mesh will not be taller than the finished box.

Construction of the Box

These boxes are heavy, and I strongly advise that you assemble them wherever their designated spot will be in your garden.

Assembly, Part 1

1. Place a 2 inch × 6 inch × 8 foot flat on the ground. Lay one 93-inch length of mesh along the top of the board, centered end to end (you should have about a 1½-inch space at each end of the board). Staple the mesh to the board at the center. Pull the mesh tight and continue stapling along the edge from the center to each end. Use lots of staples!

2. Flip the board with attached mesh over, and place one leg under each end. Make the center of the leg and the end of the board flush in each direction. Pound in one nail at each corner. You should now have a "sandwich" of board, mesh, and leg, with the mesh about 1½ inches shy of the end.

3. Flip the assembly over again. Slip another board, 2 inches × 6 inches × 8 feet, under the mesh, keeping it flush with the bottom of the legs. As before, center the mesh on this board and staple it home.

4. Flip the assembly over again (!) and place a nail at each corner. Make sure the frame is square. You can check squareness by measuring diagonally in both directions. The distances should be the same.

5. When the assembly is square, put another nail at each corner. Now staple the mesh to the two legs with lots of staples. Set the frame aside.

Now make another unit, identical to the one you just finished.

At this point, you will certainly want to take this project over to the area where it is going to be used, if you didn't start there. This puppy will be *very heavy* when completed.

Assembly, Part 2

1. Take one of the 4-foot-long end rail pieces and staple a 42-inch mesh section centered along the top edge. Stand the two long sections previously assembled in part 1 on edge, with the mesh to the inside. Nail the 4-foot piece you just stapled the mesh to across the ends of the long sides at the top. The mesh must be on the inside, and the 4-foot end will be flush with the outside of the 8-foot pieces.

2. Add the bottom 4-foot rail to the posts, and place one nail at each corner. Square the end and add a second nail at each corner.

3. Do the other end!

4. Drill and bolt each corner using two bolts through each side rail and end rail. Drill holes diagonally (not in line above each other and spaced such that the bolts don't intersect at the corners). Make it look neat! Drive the bolts in with the heads on the outside, washer and nut on the inside. Make sure the box is square before drilling holes—it's now or never!

5. Now you need to get in the box (yes, climb in it) and staple the bottom edge of the mesh along the end rails. Then staple the mesh ends to the legs.

6. Measure the distance between the top and bottom rails along the long side. Cut two pieces of 2 inch × 4 inch to this length. Center these pieces along the side and toenail them to the top and bottom rail. You might want to drill a pilot hole here to guide the nail and avoid splitting. Staple the mesh to the pieces just installed.

7. It's not necessary, but if you have a table saw available, rip some strips from the leftover 2 inch × 4 inch and nail them over the exposed mesh on the outside of the legs. This makes for a stronger box and covers the end of the mesh. You can also use 1 inch × 2 inch strips instead, or even lath, if a table saw isn't available.

8. The box is done! Now you have the fun part of filling it with straw (not hay!) and planting mix. If you're going to line the box with plastic sheeting, now is the time to do it.

Filling the Box with Straw

See figure 5.7 for an example.

You'll need the following supplies to complete this step:

- 12–13 standard straw bales per box (do not use hay!)
- 3–5 pounds ammonium sulfate or urea crystals
- hose connected to water supply

The customary way to fill the box is to obtain about 12–13 standard bales of straw, unbind them, and tear them apart. Local farmers usually sell oat or wheat straw for $1–3 per bale; urban retail garden centers may charge a bit more. Drop the straw by armfuls into the box, pack or stomp it down, and sprinkle a thin layer of ammonium sulfate or urea crystals on it, scattering them as though you were broadcasting seeds in a defined space. Then spray it liberally with water. Keep doing this; I advise filling the box in manageable, sequential layers that are about 2 feet deep each. Remember, the ammonium sulfate is important as it keeps the nitrogen in the soil, which helps the straw break down and start generating heat in a decomposing process similar to how composting works. If you or a willing helper wants to, climb up onto the straw and tromp it down as you stuff the box. This is the optimum way to pack down the straw if you don't want the top to sink down much as the season progresses.

When the box is full to the top of tightly packed straw and you've again hosed it liberally with water, I recommend one more good tromp over it on foot. We found that placing a 2 foot × 4 foot plywood scrap board under our feet really helps in packing the straw down firmly. Young folks will have a ball helping with this step. What kid can resist jumping up and down on a box full of straw? Whee!

When the box is evenly filled with straw so tightly that it feels like an extra-firm mattress when you press on it, you're ready for the planting mix. We generally put at least 6 to 8 inches of a good soil mix on the top (you can easily use a ruler to make sure the soil is deep enough), as seen in figure 5.9. Spread it out evenly, and then start either planting rows of seeds or transplanting seedlings directly into the soil. Be sure to keep the soil moist but not soaked as you begin the planting and growing process. (Please see chapter 6 for more details on this subject.)

Figure 5.8. Remember to use plain straw, not hay!
RASBAK/ WIKIMEDIA COMMONS

I should warn you that, over the season, the soil level in your big-box bed will sink down a few inches, depending upon how tightly the straw is packed, how much rainfall you've received, etc. (See fig. 5.10.) This is normal and doesn't prevent the plants from producing. At the end of each growing season (in a less-temperate climate), just remove any remaining pooped-out plants. Then, if you can or want to, you can scoop out most of the good soil and save it to use the following year. Next spring, pack more straw in the box (remember the ammonium sulfate), following the same packing, stomping, and watering process. Then add some compost and/or soil amendments to last year's soil, and start your gardening all over again.

If, however, you choose to leave the old soil in the box, that's okay, too. Just start with fresh straw the following season, using

Figure 5.9. The soil is put on top, then laced well with perlite, which will be mixed in to avoid compaction.

Figure 5.10. This raised bed wasn't packed well enough with straw before it was planted, but it still produces very well. (See next photo too.)

Figure 5.11. The straw is sinking, but the plants still thrive.   **GREG ASPINALL**

the ammonium sulfate/urea crystals, and pack the box the same way you did before. Then top it off with a fresh, new planting layer of soil on top and start your seeds or transplants.

Should you decide to get adventurous (and efficient) and decide to install micro-drip irrigation in your garden, the raised beds are perfect for it. As figure 5.12 shows, sprayer heads are easily put into place in the boxes and are especially good for the lettuces, radishes, herbs, and other plants you may grow in them. Just remember *never* to use sprayers on tomato plants, because they don't appreciate water on their foliage and will show their displeasure as they grow! Drip emitters, also used in micro-drip irrigation, are exactly right for watering tomatoes and can be used in the raised beds as well as in containers.

Figure 5.12. These sprayers are part of the micro-drip irrigation system, great for watering the raised bed.

In case you're wondering, the photo in figure 5.12 was shot in the garden of one of my "followers" who built a similar raised bed. You'll notice he used turkey wire rather than chicken wire. (See chapter 11.) His bed was at just the right stage when I needed this photo example of the micro-drip irrigation sprinklers.

Well, that's about all there is to creating this wonderful big raised bed. It should last you for many seasons and be there in the garden just like an old friend, year after year. Meanwhile, expect lots of questions and marveling from wide-eyed visitors who see it. I hope that you raise lots of tasty produce in it!

6 All About Soil and Planting

Dirt versus Soil

What's the difference between *dirt* and *soil?*

Dirt is that vague-looking, brownish substance occurring in noncultivated land areas of this planet. It's what children use, in combination with water, to create mud pies. It is the stuff that builders remove from construction sites and dispose of as fill dirt in low-lying land areas. The composition of dirt is dubious and not something you want for growing plants.

I've known individuals who decided to plant vegetable gardens using free fill dirt of questionable origin. This dirt can have anything from mostly rocks to dangerous chemicals or other substances harmful to living creatures and plants. Ix-nay on that! You may as well try to grow plants directly in concrete.

This fact was brought home to some unsuspecting, new-to-gardening folks I know who got all excited about my aboveground

methods. They quickly cobbled together the straw-bale garden and a trellis, and being on a somewhat tight budget, they checked around with friends to find some inexpensive (maybe free?) topsoil. Well, someone came through, all right, with a truckload of said "soil." When put on top of the straw in the bale garden (and in the containers designated for tomatoes and other goodies), the truth was evident. The newbie gardeners had received a truckload of construction site fill dirt! And it was just like concrete— hard, dense, and full of small gravel and other debris.

We helped them dump their filled containers and remove the nasty stuff from the bale garden. Then they had to bite the bullet and spring for something better. I'm pleased to report that, after doing so, they went on to have a very successful first-year, off-the-ground garden.

So what should you use, then? That would be soil, which is what I'd describe as a mixture of organic matter and rock fragments; it's biologically active. There are many terms used in con-

Figure 6.1. There's nothing like running your hands through a good soil mix.

junction with the various components of soil. However, unless you plan to become a soil specialist, there's no need for you to learn and memorize them all! Just a few basics will lead to you to success. To save you a trip to the library or garden center, or even from doing research on the Internet, I'll give you the essential details about the most important things you need to know about the soil to be used in your garden. You already have all of the "dirt" on dirt, right?

Soil, along with serving as a home to plant roots, also offers accommodation to microorganisms and invertebrates. Soil can be as deep as 5 feet or more, or it may be as shallow as just a few inches. Think of soil as a sponge: a complex network of varied-size pores. In fact, roughly 50 percent of soil is pore space.

A good, productive soil must be permeable so that it can supply water to plants. A soil's permeability and water-holding capacity depends on that network of pores. There are large pores, also called macropores; these control a soil's permeability and aeration (the air spaces within the soil). These macropores include earthworm and root channels. Water moves rapidly through them because of their size. This means that rainfall and irrigation infiltrate the soil, and excess water drains through it.

Micropores, on the other hand, are fine soil pores. Think tiny: Typically they are a fraction of a millimeter in diameter. They are responsible for a soil's water-holding capacity. Just like a fine-textured sponge or towel, micropores hold water against the force of gravity. A great deal of the water held in micropores will be made available to plants, but some is held so tightly that plant roots simply cannot use it.

Soil porosity includes texture, structure, compaction, and organic matter. It is important to evaluate your existing garden soil with respect to these properties to understand the part they play in the soil's porosity. Remember this particularly if you choose to grow anything directly in the ground, such as corn.

Texture describes how coarse or fine a soil is. It directly affects porosity. The coarsest soil particles are sand. These are visible to the eye and have a gritty feel. Pores between sand particles tend to be large, while those between silt and clay tend to be small. So sandy soils (mostly macropores) usually have rapid permeability but limited water-holding capacity. Micropores predominate in soils containing mostly silt and clay. This creates high water-holding capacity but reduces permeability. Silt particles are about the size of individual particles of white flour—smaller than sand.

Clay particles are the smallest, about the size of bacteria and viruses. Surprisingly, these particles can only be seen (individually) with a microscope. Soil rich in clay feels very hard when dry, but it is easily shaped and molded when moist. It's not very good by itself for growing plants.

You could say that this is a case where size matters! Almost all soils have a mixture of pore sizes. A soil with nearly equal influence from sand, silt, and clay particles is called a loam. Loams make good agricultural and garden soils because they have good water-holding capacity and moderate permeability.

A sandy loam contains more sand than a well-balanced loam. It feels gritty but has enough silt and clay to hold together in your hand. Sandy loam has low to moderate water-holding capacity and good permeability.

Silt loams, richer in silt, feel smooth rather than gritty. They're permeable when moist, but not very sticky. These loams have high water-holding capacity and low to moderate permeability.

Finally are the clay and clay loams. They are very hard when dry and sticky when wet. They can be molded into wires and ribbons when moist. Generally, clay and clay loams have high water-holding capacity and low permeability.

What does all this mean? Almost any texture of soil can be suitable for gardening—as long as you are aware of the soil's limitations. This means adjusting your management of the soil composition to compensate accordingly. Here's a summary: Clay soils hold a lot of water but are hard to dig and dry slowly in the spring. Sandy soils need more frequent watering and lighter, more frequent fertilization, but you can plant in them earlier in the spring. A good loamy mix, therefore, is ideal.

Also of concern are structure and compaction. The more dense the particles of the soil are, the more likely compaction will occur. For example, clay and other dense particles will compact more often than fine particles such as sand. Thus, the gardener needs to make sure the soil has the appropriate structure, via its composition, to avoid compaction.

All soils can benefit from additions of organic matter. It helps build and stabilize the structure in fine-textured and compacted soils. That will improve the permeability and aeration, and reduce the risk of runoff and erosion. When or-

Almost any texture of soil can be suitable for gardening—as long as you are aware of the soil's limitations.

ganic matter decomposes, it forms humus. This acts as a natural glue that binds and strengthens soil aggregates. Organic matter also helps sandy soils hold water and nutrients. It can come from various sources, which are discussed more fully in chapter 8.

If you have any knowledge of fertilizers, you've probably noted that the three primary nutrients they contain are usually abbreviated as N, P, and K, which stand for nitrogen (N), phosphorus (P), and potassium (K). If a soil's nutrient supply is deficient, fertilizers will help provide the additional nutrients needed for healthy plant growth. (This topic is more thoroughly covered in chapter 8, which focuses on composting.)

The NPK linchpins are in largest demand by plants. Secondary

nutrients are sulfur, calcium, and magnesium. These may be deficient in some soils, particularly in the Pacific Northwest. Micronutrients include zinc, iron, copper, manganese, boron, molybdenum, and chlorine. Boron deficiencies most often occur west of the Cascade Mountains, in the Northwest. Each nutrient deficiency will cause characteristic symptoms in plants. Affected plants also grow more slowly, yield less, and are less healthy than plants with adequate level of nutrients.

Is there such a thing as too many nutrients in soil? Certainly; excess nutrients can be problematic for both plants and the environment. This usually results because too much of a nutrient is applied or is applied at the wrong time. For instance, too much boron is toxic to plants, while too much nitrogen can lead to excessive foliage production. This increases the risk of disease, wind damage, and delayed flowering, fruiting, and dormancy. Nitrogen, when left in the soil at the end of the growing season, can leach into groundwater and threaten drinking water quality.

You may think that this last point won't affect you since you'll not be planting directly into the ground. However, when your containerized plants are watered, either by nature or some mechanism you arrange, there'll inevitably be runoff. That means this issue is very important when your planting mix and fertilizers are chosen. It's best to avoid excess nitrogen if you can.

The one thing you don't want in the soil for your containers or straw-bale gardens is rocks larger than the size of a pea. A few here and there aren't harmful, but in quantity or size, rocks will be a nuisance and could impede plant growth. Screening your noncommercial soil can eliminate this situation. This process involves using a big square of wire mesh, such as hardware cloth, that is framed by four pieces of wood to resemble a mesh window. Then soil is placed on this wire and brushed back and forth so that the small particles pass through the mesh and the pebbles or other unwanted large particles remain on top.

Your Growing and Planting Media

Let's assume that you're not going to use free fill dirt or other questionable stuff. You're going to either buy a premixed planting or potting soil, or, cheaper yet, mix your own. That's fine; very good. Just remember that you get what you pay for, at least to a certain point. It's not hard to drop a fortune on a premium soil or soil mix for a good-sized garden, but it may be really good stuff with a trusted brand name. Conversely, it's possible to find a cheap imitation on sale at a very low price and then find that it's just (horrors!) plain junk that won't grow anything worth mentioning. You may not notice its deficiencies right away, and that's where some knowledge of soil composition and nutrients will prove to be extremely helpful in diagnosing plant problems and amending the soil accordingly. So buyer beware: Find good brands of commercial soils and amendments and stick what you know.

Check with reputable garden centers or nurseries for their recommendations. Flip through a few gardening magazines or ask friends who garden well what they use. Notice I said "garden well"; if the friend's garden isn't very successful, he might have some soil problems. You may know someone who either raves about her great soil or rants about how awful it is. The former has good fortune; the latter will have to use soil amendments to achieve good growing conditions. If you're not putting anything directly into the ground and are going with a commercial mix or your own custom mix, this won't be an issue.

You have choices in terms of your plants: transplants/starts from nurseries and garden centers, or growing your own plants from seed. Depending on whether you're starting from seeds on a large scale or using established plants (or a combination of both), you'll need either a planting mix or a potting soil, respectively. However, a good, all-purpose mix can be used in place of potting soil and planting medium.

So you'll need to decide if you're going to purchase your planting and potting soils already mixed or if you prefer to create your
own "master mixes." The commercial, all-purpose mixes (such as
those produced by Miracle-Gro, or Sunshine, made by Sun Gro) will
usually cost about $8 for a 1-cubic-foot bag. These mixes can be
used for starting from seeds in single-plant pots, in larger grower's
pots, or in the straw-bale garden. Obviously, it can get expensive in
a hurry at $8 per bag, so you'll probably want to make your own soil
mixes. If this is the route you choose, I'd suggest buying your basic
components in large bags or 2-plus-cubic-foot bales, and then mixing them together in a large wheelbarrow, patio cement mixer,
muck tub, or other large receptacle. A large grain scoop that holds
about a quart or so will come in handy when doing this.

As it happens, I prefer to use a commercial Sunshine mix

Figure 6.2. Peat pots work very well for starting plants from seed.
CDW VICTORIA/ WIKIMEDIA COMMONS

specifically formulated for plant propagation in my greenhouse; that is called a planting mix. But for seeds sown outdoors directly in the soil in my containers and the straw-bale gardens, I use an all-purpose mix that I make. Whether you purchase it ready to use or mix up your own is up to you.

For my outdoors, all-purpose mix, I have great luck with using about six parts of a basic, generic topsoil or planting soil, one part peat moss, two parts aged or sterile steer manure, and one large grain scoop of perlite or vermiculite. Bear in mind that fresh bovine (cow) manure cannot be immediately used in any planting mix. That's because it can carry disease-causing pathogens and has to age for several months to a year before use. (See chapter 8 on composting.)

Depending on the quantity of mix you make, it should give you enough to fill quite a few large grower's containers and might even start a good layer on the straw-bale garden. With the commercial-mix bag, however, you'll only get a handful of containers' worth. It may simply be more convenient and feel more goof-proof to go with commercial mixes, however, and that's perfectly all right to do.

If you plan to do your own composting (see chapter 8), you'll still need some fertilizer for the first year. You can readily purchase good mixed fertilizers for annual gardens; pick an 8-8-8 or 10-20-20 blend (these are N-P-K ratios). Fertilizer blends for starting plants usually have a higher proportion of phosphorus. Avoid lawn fertilizers, which are much higher in nitrogen than the other two nutrients. Follow the directions as to the amount to add for the correct ratio of fertilizer to soil mix. If, by chance, you already have compost that's ready to use, add a couple of scoops of that to your mix.

See table 6.1, which has plants grouped according to their nutrient needs. While it doesn't include absolutely every plant you might grow, it covers the majority and most commonly grown vegetables.

Table 6.1. Nutrient needs of plants

Heavy feeders	Light feeders	Soil builders
Asparagus	Carrot	Alfalfa
Beet	Garlic	Bean, broad
Broccoli*	Leek	Bean, lima
Brussels sprout	Mustard	Bean, snap
Cabbage*	Onion	Clover
Cantaloupe*	Parsnip	Pea
Cauliflower	Pepper	Peanut
Celery	Potato	Soybean
Collard	Rutabaga	
Corn	Shallot	
Cucumber*	Sweet potato	
Eggplant	Swiss chard	
Endive	Turnip	
Kale		
Kohlrabi		
Lettuce		
Okra		
Parsley		
Pumpkin*		
Radish		
Rhubarb		
Spinach		
Squash, summer*		
Squash, winter*		
Sunflower		
Tomato*		
Watermelon*		

*Fertilize a minimum of two times

Starting Seeds

Should you decide to do your own plant propagation indoors from scratch, you have options. (For setting out already-developed plants—also referred to as transplants—skip this and jump ahead to the "Transplants" section.) You can use cells or minipots set into flats just as growers and I do. You can also grow seedlings in premade wooden or plastic flats and trays, or you can make them from scrap lumber. An important point: The planting mix for propagating seeds indoors differs from that used outdoors for containers and the raised beds. Both are similar, but there are a few important differences.

Many different kinds of planting media can be used to start seeds. They include "grower's mix"; vermiculite alone or mixed in with other soilless, artificial materials; and various amended soil mixes. Regardless of what material is used, a growing (germinating) medium must meet these criteria:

- Be fine and uniform, yet well aerated and loose
- Be free of insects, disease organisms, and weed seeds
- Be low in fertility and total soluble salts
- Be capable of holding and removing moisture by capillary action (holding just the right amount of moisture, yet maintaining good drainage)

A great mixture that has all of these attributes is a combination of one-third pasteurized soil; one-third sand, vermiculite, or perlite; and one-third sphagnum peat moss. Be sure that you never use general garden soil (i.e., your custom planting mix) to start seedlings in propagation cells or pots. It is not sterile, is too heavy, doesn't drain well, and shrinks from the sides of containers if allowed to dry out. There are excellent starter mixes available.

I like the Sunshine #1 Mix or the Sunshine Professional Growing

Mix (both made by Sun Gro), but that's just my personal preference. Either of these are already sterile when purchased and can
be used directly from the bag. However, bear in mind that I grow
quite a lot of plants from seed every year—flowers, herbs, and vegetables—and I have a greenhouse. For more modest endeavors,
here's where you can catch a break: An artificial, soilless mix does
not need to be sterilized. A mix such as sphagnum peat moss and
vermiculite is generally free of diseases, weed seed, and insects.
These materials are readily available, easy to handle, lightweight,
and able to produce uniform plant growth.

Other ready-made soilless (peatlike) mixes or similar products are commercially available. Or they can be made at home.
To do so, thoroughly mix together the following ingredients:

- 4 quarts shredded sphagnum peat moss
- 4 quarts fine-grade vermiculite
- 1 tablespoon superphosphate
- 2 tablespoons ground limestone

Here's a second recipe:

- 50 percent vermiculite or perlite
- 50 percent milled sphagnum peat moss with fertilizer

Unfortunately, these mixes have little fertility, so you must
water seedlings with a diluted fertilizer solution soon after they
sprout.

Using sterile pots or cells is essential, too—and easy. Simply
wash them with clean water into which about one-half cup of chlorine bleach has been added. This will effectively kill any pathogens
that could be lurking in the pot. Larger pots and other growing containers should be thoroughly clean, too. First, wash them to remove
debris, then use the bleach water to rinse them. (This, incidentally,

is a good action to take with any container you're using for the first time, especially those you may have purchased at yard sales, gotten at recycling centers, or received from friends.) Be sure to avoid re-contaminating the planting medium (soil) and tools.

Remember: Don't use soil from an existing garden to start seeds! It contains highly destructive disease organisms that can kill small plants. However, if you have no choice and cannot purchase a commercial seed-starting mix, you can pasteurize that garden soil first in an oven. Place slightly moist soil into a heat-resistant container, cover it, and bake it in a 250°F oven. You can use a candy or meat thermometer to make sure the mix reaches 140°F for at least 30 minutes. Overheating can damage the soil, so keep an eye on it. Following this procedure will, however, prevent damping off and other plant diseases, and it will also eliminate potential plant pests. Be aware that some very unpleasant odors can result from this, so if you have an outdoor oven, you may want to use that instead of your in-house kitchen oven.

Sowing dates generally range from 4 to 12 weeks prior to the last spring frost.

When to plant seeds? That's the question! For sowing seeds indoors, the proper time depends on when the resulting transplants may be safely moved outdoors. This depends greatly upon your geographic location. Sowing dates generally range from 4 to 12 weeks prior to the last spring frost. Of course, this depends on the cold hardiness of the plant, speed of germination, rate of growth, and conditions provided. It's common to make the mistake of sowing seeds too early and then trying to hold seedlings back under poor light or improper temperature. Usually the result will be tall, weak, spindly plants that won't do well in the garden. Check with your extension service or a reputable garden center to find out

when to start indoor seedlings in your particular geographic region. Seed packets, too, usually carry such planting specifics.

There's quite a bit of variation in seed size, soil type, and seasons that influence the depth in which seeds should be covered. Light is required for some seeds to germinate; these should not be covered at all. Follow the directions on each specific seed packet for planting instructions. It will give you the recommended lateral seed spacing, soil depth, thinning instructions, etc. These instructions will apply to seeds planted both indoors and out-of-doors.

The big essential in starting seeds indoors is adequate light. More people lose their homegrown seedlings to inadequate light than to any other factors. Grown under low-light conditions, seedlings are leggy and weak. They will topple over when 3 to 4 inches tall. So unless you are blessed with a sunny room or porch that has a southern exposure, you'll need supplemental light. This isn't a tough issue; a fluorescent shop light with two cool white bulbs will get the job done. These two bulbs will illuminate a width of 12 inches along their length, although light intensity falls off at both ends. The bulbs should be replaced yearly.

You have several options for seed-starting containers:

- **Preformed pellets or cubes.** These must be soaked until thoroughly wet, and then plant the seeds in the holes provided. You can then plant the whole cube in your container or straw-bale garden without disturbing the plant's roots.
- **Flats or other large containers** (as illustrated in fig. 6.3). Seedlings planted in these should be grown until they have one or two sets of true leaves. Then transplant them into individual containers and grow them to full transplant size. You've got plenty of economical options here: pots, old cans, cut-off milk cartons, margarine tubs, or other old throwaways or recyclables.

- **Pop-out trays.** Easy to use and reusable, these are available at garden centers.
- **Peat pots.** Large seeds and herbs are good candidates for these. You can sow one or two large seeds, or several small seeds, directly into each peat pot. Thin these to one or two seedlings per pot. These peat pots can be planted directly into your grower's pots or other growing areas.

No matter which seed-starting container you use, fill your selected pots or trays to three-quarters full with planting medium (the growing mix). For tiny seeds, the top ¼ inch should be a layer of fine, screened mix or vermiculite. This makes it easier for the

Figure 6.3. Open trays as well as those with compartments can be used to start plants from seed.

little fellas to break through and sprout up. Sow the seeds (see fig. 6.4), covering them (or not, according to instructions) to the specified depth, and then add enough water to moisten the soil. Don't overwater or fill up the containers, or the seed might float right up to the top and be lost.

If your home is dry, I suggest that you cover the containers or trays with plastic wrap. This will help maintain a consistent moisture level until the seeds germinate; seeds and seedlings are very sensitive to drying out. However, keeping them soaking wet is not good, either, because constant moisture encourages damping off, a fungal disease that's deadly to seedlings. This tendency can be reduced by sprinkling milled sphagnum moss, which contains a natural fungicide, directly on top of the soil.

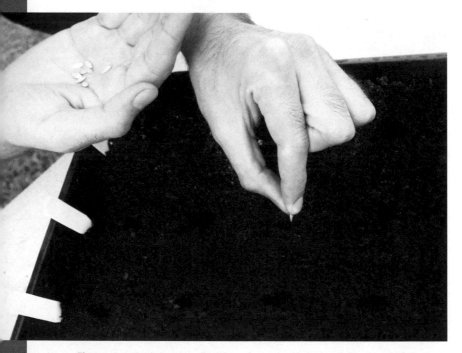

Figure 6.4. Patience is called for when planting those tiny seeds, but it pays off!

How to know what to grow is, well, it's up to you. Have you selected the types and varieties of plants you want—tomatoes, peppers, herbs, etc.? Within these families of plants, you'll find choices ranging from the size of the plant to the length of the plant's growing season and production limitations. For instance, tomatoes can be of the determinate type (meaning that the plant will produce a set amount of fruit and then stop) or an indeterminate, which means the

Live dangerously and try something new: Perhaps a striped tomato or different-colored squash would be fun.

plant will continue producing indefinitely and/or until the first frost of fall. Choosing to use disease-resistant varieties means less grief when the growing season starts.

Be sure to obtain some seed catalogs from reputable companies or visit their websites to check out their offerings. For four-season climate residents, this annual task is good to do in late winter, when it's still too cold to do any planting. (If by chance you forget something while placing your order, you can always purchase reliable seeds locally when your area's planting season starts.) Flip through those catalogs and see what catches your eye. Interesting vegetable and herb varieties—whether heirloom or hybrid, determinate or indeterminate—are fun to try. Live dangerously and try something new: Perhaps a striped tomato or different-colored squash would be fun. Check with garden-buff friends for their recommendations. You may discover a new variety of heirloom tomato or some other intriguing item that you've never seen before in your local grocery stores or farmer's markets.

Unrealistic expectations about growing warm-zone plants in a cooler climate usually means disappointment down the road. Seed catalogs and websites will include grower's recommendations for various planting zones across the country, but it's also helpful to checking around at local farmer's markets and other grower outlets. This way you can see what the winners and losers are in the local vegetable-growing arena.

Planting Seeds Directly in Containers or Straw-Bale Gardens

You can sow just about any seeds directly into containers; just follow the directions as for planting in peat pots. See table 6.2 for how many seeds to plant in containers. It is divided for grower's pots and dishpans used as planters.

Table 6.2. Number of seeds to plant per container type

Dishpans	Seeds per pan	Grower's pots	Seeds per pot
Cucumbers	4	Beets	12
Melons	4	Bok choy	8–10
Peas	8–10	Broccoli	1
Pole beans	6–8	Carrots	15
Squash	4	Cauliflower	1
		Eggplant*	2
		Herbs	6–8
		Leeks	3–4
		Lettuce	10–15
		Peppers (bell and chili)*	3–4
		Spinach	10–15
		Swiss chard	5–6

* These also do well in straw-bale gardens.

If you build and use the straw-bale raised beds, you can plant seeds directly into them in any direction you choose. My beds are the 8 foot × 4 foot × 3 foot beds shown in chapter 5. I usually plant them across the 4-foot width in rows, but you could choose to plant them down the length, instead, and that would be fine. Just make sure you leave enough space between rows of plants that will bush out, like lettuce, herbs, peppers, etc.

Transplants

If you're not into growing plants from seed, you can always pick up the desired plants from a bona fide plant nursery and/or real garden center. Those are my vendors of choice. It's true that big-box retailers, home centers, hardware stores, and other retailers often carry plants in addition to their other merchandise. However, experience has taught me to shy away from buying from them. In our region last year, for instance, there were problems with diseases such as early and late tomato blight that were ultimately traced to such vendors.

Only scrupulous sanitation controls and practices will prevent such diseases from happening and spreading. They can easily slide by the attention of large-scale growing operations such as those supplying the all-inclusive, multidepart-

A word of caution: Don't even think about trying to transplant beans, peas, okra, and radishes!

ment stores. So be very leery of cut-rate prices on plants and, if you do decide to chance it, look them over very carefully for early signs of disease or weakness before buying them.

A word of caution: Don't even think about trying to transplant beans, peas, okra, and radishes! Review table 6.3 to see which plants can be transplanted with best success, as far as the standard wisdom goes. I would *never* try transplanting carrots or lettuce, for instance; they both germinate and grow fairly readily when planted as seeds. Their delicate structure as seedlings makes me too nervous to risk their demise during the transplanting process!

Table 6.3. Transplantability of vegetable plants

Easily survive	Require care	Not successful*
Broccoli	Beet	Bean
Brussels sprout	Carrot (young)	Okra
Cabbage	Celery	Pea
Cauliflower	Chard	Radish
Chinese cabbage	Corn	
Eggplant	Cucumber	
Leek	Melon	
Lettuce	Squash	
Onion (tends to bolt)		
Pepper		
Tomato		

*Using customary methods

I will not delve into the process of setting out perennial plants or crowns such as asparagus. You can easily find such information from your extension service or other online information source.

Don't forget the importance of location! If you're this far into the book, I'm going to assume that you have read the previous chapters and determined where you're going to place your containers and other off-ground gardening components. And I hope you've chosen containers appropriately sized to the plants that will occupy them. A robust tomato plant needs a 3- to 5-gallon grower's pot in order to be prolific and happy. The same rule applies to bush beans, beets, turnips, carrots, etc.

Setting Out Transplants

Your annual vegetable transplants are ideally stocky, healthy, free from disease, and have good roots. While they should have a few sets of true leaves, they shouldn't be too mature. Yellow, woody, or already flowering plants fit into that category. Often, after transplanting, flowers or immature fruits will drop. If you've had the plants indoors since seeding them, or if they've been luxuriating in a greenhouse, they must be hardened off so that they can easily adapt to environmental change. This means setting them outside during the day and bringing them in at night over a period of several days. There must be no danger of low temperatures or frost when you begin transplanting them outdoors.

Figure 6.5. Young beets and other plants are doing well.   GREG ASPINALL

Ready to set them out? Try doing your transplanting on a shady day, in late afternoon or in early evening. This will prevent wilting. Water plants several hours in advance before transplanting. Never let them dry out completely at any time! Handle the plants carefully and avoid bruising their stems or disturbing the roots.

I prefer to keep the plants hydrated with water mixed with a transplanting solution; good brands include Miracle-Gro Quick Start and Bonide Plant Starter Concentrate, or you might be lucky enough to find jugs of B-1 Starter Solution. Whichever you choose, follow the directions for mixing with water. You can also make your own starter solution with half strength fish fertilizer, fish emulsion, or manure tea. Another good starter solution is 1 tablespoon fish emulsion plus 1 tablespoon liquid seaweed to 1 gallon

Figure 6.6. This very healthy specimen is ready to be transplanted.
LYN LOMASI/ WIKIMEDIA COMMONS

of water. Have one of these solutions ready before you start the transplanting process.

I like to use an old dinner fork to pry hearty seedlings from their growing containers, but this must be done carefully. Be sure to keep the fork vertical until it strikes the bottom, and then gently pull up on it, bringing up the entire root ball and plant together. Or, instead of using a fork, you can carefully tip the container sideways or upside down and gently squeeze it to loosen the soil and plants (See fig. 6.6).

In the receiving container or raised bed, use a trowel to dig a hole wider and slightly deeper than the root ball. After placing the transplant into that hole, pour about 1 cup of starter solution in the hole around the plant. Then fill the remainder of the hole with soil, taking care to press it firmly around the plant's roots.

Depending on the windiness of your surroundings, you may want to protect transplants for a few days. You can place newspaper or cardboard on their south sides, or cover them with open-weave baskets or clear plastic jugs. (The jugs should have their bottoms cut off, and then one can be carefully placed over each plant.) Floating row cover is also an excellent protective material. White, thin, and clothlike, it is sold in long lengths. When stretched over rows of plants, it lets the light through while protecting plants from cold temperatures. It is sold by most grower's supply establishments and some garden centers.

Watering

Plants must have adequate moisture for good growth. Did you know that a healthy plant is 75 to 90 percent water? That life-giving liquid is used for the plant's vital functions. These include photosynthesis, support (rigidity), and transport of nutrients and sugars. During the first two weeks of growth, water is also used by plants to build their root systems.

Be sure to water the transplanted young'uns once or twice during the first week if there is insufficient rain. Keep 'em moist, but avoid soaking deeply. When plants are established (after about one week), whether watering by hand or via micro-drip irrigation, you must adhere to a schedule at the plant's convenience—not yours! This fact is often what it takes to convince a person to put in a micro-drip irrigation system. (See chapter 7.) It automates the watering task and ensures that each plant receives just the right amount of moisture delivered directly to the plant when needed. Regardless of your watering method choice, you'll want to check table 6.4 to learn the critical moisture periods for the most common vegetables.

Table 6.4. Critical moisture periods for popular vegetables	
Crop	**Growth period**
Bean	During flowering and pod development
Broccoli and related cole crops	During head formation and enlargement
Cucumber	During flowering and fruit development
Eggplant	During blossom set through fruit enlargement
Onion	During bulb formation
Pea	During flowering and pod filling
Pepper	From blossom set through fruit enlargement
Potato	After initial tubers form
Tomato	From blossom set through fruit enlargement

From April to September, vegetables need about 1 inch of water a week. The amount will vary depending upon weather and growth stages. During dry periods, you'll need to provide a thorough weekly watering of 1 to 2 inches. Water for a depth of 5 to 6 inches, or to the root depth. Most garden soils will store about 2 to 4 inches of water per foot of depth, although the storage capacity depends on the type of soil you're using. Don't water again until the top few inches begin to dry out. You can easily test the soil moisture by poking a finger into the soil; this is the most efficient way to monitor water needs.

How much water is ideal? Well, frequent light watering encourages shallow rooting. Plants growing under those conditions will suffer more during droughts and not be as strong. On the other hand, too much water in poorly drained soils or containers deprives plants of oxygen—and they drown! Seedlings obviously need more frequent water, at a shallower depth. Mature plants need deeper water, but less frequently.

If using micro-drip irrigation (chapter 7), you'll have control over the amount of water delivered to each plant via emitters or sprayers of various capacities. Timers take the guesswork out of it, or you can simply schedule yourself a time to turn on the system each day.

No matter what watering method you use, be sure to adjust the amount of water in the event of prolonged heavy rain or extended hot, dry weather.

Well, I expect that your brain is quite full now, probably whirling with all kinds of thoughts about the choices you will be making about soil, planting, watering, and so forth as you learn how wonderful it is to stand up and garden with these new-to-you methods. So let's not chicken out now—after you take a break, move on to chapter 7 and find out how easy it is to lay out and use micro-drip irrigation!

7
Installing a Micro-Drip Irrigation System

DOES THIS SOUND LIKE a complex, scary thing—providing water to your garden without holding a hose or setting out a sprinkler? Don't be afraid, and don't just move on to the next chapter! If I, a woman in her 60s with no plumbing skills, can design, lay out, and connect a micro-drip irrigation system, so can you. And when you're finished and turn on the water supply, you'll feel an incredible sense of accomplishment—you really did it!

Friends and neighbors will brag about you, their clever friend whose garden is all watered by a self-installed micro-drip irrigation system. If they want to learn how it's done, either buy or loan them a copy of this book. On second thought, better make it a purchased copy, or you'll may never see the loaned one again—they might just decide to "stand up and garden" all the way!

Let's start with the basics and the excellent reasons for using a micro-drip irrigation system. Water is an essential component of gardening, be it flowers or vegetables. As water resources are often limited in many geographic areas, keeping plants irrigated becomes problematic. It is also very time consuming and troublesome to stand in place, hand-watering a garden. Simply setting out a sprinkler or soaker hose to water a garden plot isn't the answer, either. It wastes a great deal of water with a hit-and-miss application and causes water to linger on foliage of some plants. On tomatoes, and cucurbits (squash, melon, and cucumbers) particularly, this creates potential for disease and spoilage.

Plants develop and "drink" through their root zones. To avoid stress, plants should receive sufficient water to keep the root zone moist but not saturated. A proper balance of air and water avoids a soaked/parched cycle created by conventional watering methods. The result is healthier plants with optimum growth.

Figure 7.1. Carrots receive a daily drink from the irrigation dripper.
GREG ASPINALL

Did you know that micro-drip irrigation will reduce your water usage and evaporation by up to 70 percent? Another bonus is that weeds won't receive the water, only the root zone of the designated plants. With no runoff, soil erosion won't occur, as water is applied exactly at the rate that the soil can accept it.

Can micro-drip irrigation be used on hillsides? You bet! It can be buried or left aboveground year-round. Personally, I prefer to place the watering system aboveground, laying it out on the surface from the water source to the plants. The connection is simpler, with no need for risers and other considerations inherent with underground installations. Due to our harsh winters, I have no need for the system then, so I pick it all up and store it away until the next growing season. But what if your garden is a long distance from the faucet? That's okay. Even if you must run 100 feet of hose, this will work with micro-drip irrigation systems.

So what have you already learned? It should be that installing a micro-drip irrigation system is a simple, do-it-yourself project that will reduce your water bill and save you time. Less hand watering and easier garden maintenance means a happier gardener and higher yields of vegetables—a winning situation all around! Gardening is "green" to begin with, and reducing your energy requirements further with lower operating pressure means that you're contributing to the good of the Earth. This is a great bonus for pump-driven water systems. By using an automatic electronic timer, watering occurs at the best time of day for maximum absorption and minimal evaporation, too.

Designing Your Drip System

Let's take a look at some of the things you'll want to consider in designing your drip system. Certain words and terms used in this chapter to describe system components, operation, and physical parts can be referenced in the glossary of terms at this chapter's

end. You may wish, in fact, to peruse the glossary first to familiarize yourself with the terms before reading this chapter. Another good source of information is garden centers and agricultural supply stores, which stock manufacturers' booklets that illustrate basic equipment and typical layouts. Perhaps the next time you're out running errands, you can stop in and pick one up.

You don't need a huge amount of hardware to get started. First, unless you are going to dedicate a water faucet for use only with the drip system, you'll want a splitter. This device is shaped like a Y and allows for two separate hoses to be connected to the same faucet. It should be the kind that has a separate valve handle on each side so the water supply can be turned on and off manually. Splitters cost about $5 and are simply screwed directly onto the faucet spigot. From there you can add a timer, an antisiphon device (or backflow preventer), a pressure regulator, a filter, a swivel hose adaptor, the main line, branch lines, and watering devices (emitters, sprayers, etc.). (See fig. 7.2 for a picture of the complete assembly, mounted on a faucet.) The aforementioned components are connected to a water source by a single valve and work together to supply water to all or one of your plant groups.

Timers are optional and are great to have, but they aren't essential as long as you remember to turn the water on at the desired time each day. Another shortcoming of turning the valve on and off manually is that, sometimes we all forget to turn the valve off—like for 24 hours! So a timer will pay for itself the first year.

Fortunately, many drip irrigation suppliers are just a click away on the Internet. Most of them carry a very reasonably priced basic/starter kit, which includes all of the aforementioned components and instructions for assembling everything. Extra parts are readily available in individual or bulk quantities. You'll find a list of suppliers at the end of this chapter.

When you place your order, be sure to purchase a hole punch and a cutting tool. A hole punch, a little handheld device with a

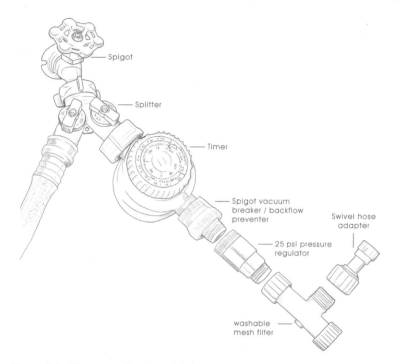

Spigot

Splitter

Timer

Spigot vacuum
breaker / backflow
preventer

Swivel hose
adapter

25 psi pressure
regulator

washable
mesh filter

Figure 7.2. These are the essential drip irrigation parts that fit sequentially onto the water source, usually a faucet.

tapered point, is used to make a precise hole in main line tubing to install emitters or transfer barbs. When using this punch, you'll simply squeeze the sides of the tubing with your hand and push on the punch while giving a slight twist. You will usually hear a pop. Because heat will soften the tubing, it is easier to punch holes at cooler times of the day, or by running cold water through the tubing first. The cutting tool, on the other hand, is a very sharp razor device used to cut the ½-inch tubing. You hold the tool in one hand, place the tubing exactly where you want to make a cut, and squeeze the handle. Works great! Both the hole punch and cutting tool are very inexpensive, but they are essential. They are carried by most of the drip system parts vendors.

Time for a quick review. In its simplest form, the system starts

at a faucet, then progresses through a timer, antisiphon, pressure regulator, filter, tubing, and emitters or sprayers. (Of course, you don't have to use a timer, but I certainly recommend one.) A filter should be used on all drip systems to prevent emitter clogging. A pressure regulator is generally recommended, though not always necessary, depending on the water pressure and type of emitters and/or sprayers you are using. Again, talking directly with any of the drip system vendors is very helpful in getting it right the first time.

While most drip systems start at a faucet, it is also possible to start off from a buried PVC line. This can provide a larger water flow and allows you to tap into the same line at several points with either ½-inch or ¾-inch poly tubing. Generally, when this is done, a manifold with one or more electric valves is used to control the watering zones. An electric timer is connected to the valves to control when the zone is turned on or off. This is a higher-end system than the type that will be discussed here; however, most drip system manufacturers carry a full line of valves and timers, and can help you design a system of this type.

Bear in mind that there is almost always more than one way to achieve a successful system.

Bear in mind that there is almost always more than one way to achieve a successful system. Sometimes it may seem that there are too many choices, but keep in mind that drip is forgiving and can usually be modified if something isn't quite right the first time. Adding on to a system can be as simple a popping a couple of emitters into an existing line to water a new planting, or it may involve splitting one zone into two, if more water is required than is available using the existing tubing all in one zone.

When starting to design your drip system hardware and layout, there are a few basic things that you will want to know. The first is how much water you have available, what is referred to as the water flow. Take a container (5 gallons is a good size) and time how long it takes to fill at the faucet where you want to start your drip system. If the bucket fills in one minute, then your flow is 300 gallons per hour (gph). As ½-inch tubing can only carry 250 gph, you could attach a splitter (hose Y) and run two separate systems off that faucet using the usual ½-inch poly tubing main line. For other size containers and flow rate, go to the handy Dripworks calculator (www.dripworks.com/tutorial.php) and plug in the container size and the time it took to fill, and it will give you the flow in gallons per hour. (Or see *Flow* in the glossary at the end of the chapter for directions on how to calculate this yourself.) Make a note of this number for future reference.

The water pressure is also something useful to know. If you have high water pressure (i.e., more than 40 pounds per square inch [psi]), you'll probably want a regulator on the system. Pressure gauges that measure water pressure are available, and you may be able to get one at your local hardware store. Regulators are inexpensive ($7–12) and can protect your system from having tubing come out of fittings due to high pressure. A rate of 25 to 30 psi will be adequate (and is desirable) to run your drip-system watering devices. You can run a total volume of up to 250 gph on a single ½-inch tubing circuit.

The total amount of plain ½-inch tubing should be limited to 200 to 300 feet, which will cover a very generously sized garden area. A single length of ¼-inch tubing running to a single plant or grouping (for sprayers) should be limited to 30 feet. Again, this will be quite adequate for most garden layouts. I usually have some 75 tomato plants set out, each on its own dripper, and another 30 to 50 containerized miscellaneous plants configured the same way. Depending upon my time and what's growing in the straw-bale gardens, I will run a separate main line (the ½-inch tubing) out to them and use micro-tubing and emitters or sprayers right up on their surfaces. (See fig 5.12 for an example of this.)

Another important consideration is the type of soil you have. However, when you are gardening in containers and high raised beds, you'll be using a good mix of soil (I hope!) that won't tend heavily to either clay or sand. This means less effort will be needed when determining the spacing and flow of emitters. In-ground gardening requires more considerations and planning, and we will leave that to the nonstanding gardeners!

By growing vegetables in the methods described herein, you probably won't want or need to break it up into too many areas or "zones." To keep things simple, do plan to group your plantings that have similar water frequency and quantity requirements. This will make it easy to have all of those similar plants on the same watering line. On the other hand, if you have many different types of plants that need different amounts of water but can be watered on the same schedule, you can use higher flow emitters or sprayers on the thirstier plants and lower flow emitters on the thriftier plants to balance the system.

Another consideration in deciding how many zones you need is the amount of water required for all of the plants in a particular zone. Main line poly tubing is available in ½-inch and ¾-inch diameters. Branch line tubing comes in ¼-inch. This can go to ¼-inch soaker drip line, individual emitters, or sprayers. An estimate is that the ½-inch tubing can carry around 250 gph, and the ¾-inch tubing can carry 480 gph. I use the ½-inch tubing. By estimating how many plants you wish to water this way, and what size emitters you want to use, you'll be able to see your water requirement and check if the tubing will carry that amount of water. If you set things up and then find that your plants are not getting enough water, you can always increase the amount of time that they are watered to give them more volume. As stated before, drip irrigation systems are pretty flexible and respond well to adjustments.

Laying Out Your Drip System

You may do whatever you please in laying out your garden, choosing exactly where you set your containers, trellises, raised beds, etc. Having said that, if you think you might want to try using micro-drip irrigation, I do suggest that you place your containers in rows appropriately spaced for plant growth. I usually have four long rows of plants in my main large-container grouping. They are organized by type of plant—i.e., all of the tomatoes are grouped together with the approximately same amount of spacing per plant. This makes it easy to configure the micro tubing, barbs, and emitters to serve plants in pairs if desired. (See fig. 7.3.)

In addition to all of my large containers, my garden has four trellises with the dishpans beneath them, and three of the big raised beds. All of these structures sit atop a commercial weed barrier to make for clean, easy installation and maintenance—to say nothing of eliminating unwanted weeds and grass.

Figure 7.3. The water source (green garden hose) literally "tees" into the half-inch tubing, which accommodates the micro-tubing lengths that bring water to each individual plant.   GREG ASPINALL

I usually lay out two ½-inch main lines, via a T-shaped device inserted at the garden end of the water supply hose, to go through the large container groupings. (See fig. 7.4.) Each of those ½-inch tubings stretches along the length of the rows of plants, and then I use the hole punch to stick in the double-pointed barbs. I use ¼-inch micro tubing to deliver the water, through emitters, to each plant. If I miscalculated and need extra holes and micro tubing lines, it's easy to punch another one wherever it's needed. What about too many holes? There are little "goof" plugs available, and I always keep a supply on hand!

Next I clamp off the end of one of the two main lines. Using a joining tube on the other line's end, I then stick another long, uncut length of the ½-inch main line tubing into that and snake it along the ground, under the center of the trellises and out the

Figure 7.4. Each plant has an individual length of micro-tubing that fastens into the half-inch tubing. Then a drip emitter on the other end provides the water to the plant.   GREG ASPINALL

other end, where I cut and clamp off the end of that ½-inch tubing. Finally, I use the hole punch again to insert barbs wherever I want them and attach micro tubing and emitters accordingly.

Now, don't be intimidated; it's not nearly as complex as it sounds! Drip system suppliers will provide you with drawings of typical system layouts and can advise you as to any specific needs you don't see addressed in the literature. If you have a computer (or can use one at a public library), go online and take a look at some of the following sources of micro-drip irrigation supplies:

- Dripworksusa.com
- Irrigationdirect.com
- Sprinklerwarehouse.com
- Dripirrigation.com
- Dripdepot.com

These websites provide definitions, explanations, artwork, and photographs to help clarify the whole process. Or you can do as suggested earlier in this chapter—go to a well-supplied garden center or agricultural supply store and pick up a booklet on micro-drip irrigation. This really isn't rocket science, and *you can do it.*

Good luck, and happy, effortless watering!

Glossary of Micro-Drip Irrigation Terms

Branch line. Polyethylene tubing that attaches to the main line to bring water to a plant or to an area of a zone. Branch tubing is generally ¼-inch or ½-inch tubing.

Drip vs. ***spray.*** Emitters, or sprayers, are the pieces that actually distribute the water from your tubing to your plants. Suppliers carry a wide range of emitters, sprayers, minisprinklers, and misters. Personal preference and plant water needs determine which to choose. Emitters or spray heads can be inserted directly into the main line or can be attached to ¼-inch micro tubing for placement away from the main line.

Drippers are the best choice for low-pressure situations, individual plants, or for plants that won't tolerate water on the foliage. Sprayers are good for evenly wetting larger areas and for increasing humidity around moisture-loving plants. Sprayers are also useful in areas where you want to minimize the amount of tubing visible in your plantings or where it's too difficult to lay emitter tubing or soaker drip line. Sprayers and minisprinklers tend to put out much more water than drippers, but they are still water saving compared to traditional sprinkler systems.

Elevation. Variations in elevation can cause a change in water pressure within the system. Pressure changes by 1 pound for every 2.3 feet of change in elevation, or roughly 4 pounds of pressure for every 10 feet of change in vertical elevation. If you lose too much pressure, then the emitters at the end of the line may put out little, if any, water. If your water source is much higher than your garden, then you may need to use one or more pressure regulators to bring the pressure down to a level that drip prefers.

Emitter. An emitter, also called a dripper, is a product used in drip irrigation to regulate the flow from the main line or branch line tubing to the area to be irrigated. Emitters can be placed in the main line or branch line, at the end of ¼-inch branch line, or preinstalled inside emitter tubing.

Filter. A filter is used to remove particles from the water that might otherwise plug up your emitters. The size of the filter screen is expressed as mesh, with larger numbers denoting smaller openings in the screen. In drip irrigation, 155 and 200 mesh are common sizes. Y filters, T filters and in-line filters are the basic filters recommended for most home drip systems. Filters are placed at the faucet or just after the timer.

Fitting. A part such as an elbow, T, hose beginning, hose end, coupler, or other piece used to connect tubing. Fittings are used on the main line tubing to shape it and to make connections. The most common fittings are female hose beginnings, ends, elbows, T's, and couplers. Fittings can be compression, barbed, or "easy loc." Compression fittings hold well up to 70 psi and are inexpensive, but they can be difficult to install and remove. Barbed fittings require the use of clamps to hold them in place and are used with flat tube, poly tube above ¾ inch, and Aquapore. Easy loc fittings are easiest to use and are suitable for most home applications; ¼-inch micro fittings attach micro tubing to the main line and can also be used to branch off along a ¼-inch run.

Flow (gph or gpm). The amount of water available for the system. It is expressed as either gph (gallons per hour) or gpm (gallons per minute). Flow is measured by timing how long it takes to fill a container of a given size with the faucet opened up all the way. To calculate the gallons per minute, you can either use a flow calculator or use the following formula: (1) Divide the size of the container (in gallons) by the number of seconds to fill the container. (2) Multiply that number by 3,600. (3) Divide that number by 60.

Your flow will play a big part in determining how many plants (or how large an area) can be watered at one time. If your garden needs more water than the flow available, you can divide the drip system into as many zones (or hydro zones) as necessary. A multizone timer will allow you to schedule each zone for a different start time and duration of watering.

Friction loss. As water moves through tubing, pressure is lost due to friction in the line. In tubing runs of more than 200 feet, there can be a significant drop in pressure that can lower the output of some (non–pressure compensating) emitters or sprayers at the end of the line. Friction loss can increase if the tubing goes uphill or decrease if it goes downhill. To decrease friction, a larger size of tubing can be used.

Hydro zone. A hydro zone describes a group of plants that needs watering at a similar frequency. For example, if you have shrubs and trees, you may want to water the shrubs every other day and the trees once every two weeks. This would not be possible within a single hydro zone. Establishing two hydro zones, one for the trees and one for the shrubs, would allow you to water the two groups to their individual needs. Within a hydro zone, if one plant needs more water than another, it can be given an additional emitter or an emitter with a larger flow.

Main line. Polyethylene tubing used to carry the water from your water supply to your system. There are two commonly used sizes: ½ inch and ¾ inch. The ½-inch main line tubing has a capacity of around 240 gph. The ¾-inch main line tubing has a capacity of around 480 gph. For systems with higher water requirements, ¾-inch poly tubing (up to about 480 gph) or 1-inch-plus flat tube can be used. Use a hole punch to make holes in the main line for emitters or transfer barbs, or cut the tubing with scissors or pruning shears to attach fittings.

Manifold. A collection of valves and associated parts used to distribute water to multiple zones.

Pressure (psi). Pressure is the force pushing the water flow. Pressure is expressed in pounds per square inch (psi). A pressure regulator can be used to reduce pressure to a range that works well with the particular products you are using. If you are using pressure compensating emitter tubing, emitters, or sprayers, the range of pressure can usually be between 10 and 50 psi and still provide an even watering to your garden. If you have low pressure, you may need to use non–pressure compensating emitters or other products that can operate with very little water pressure.

Pressure compensating. Describes an emitter or sprayer that delivers a consistent amount of water over a specified range of pressures. This is useful in situations where the tubing runs are long or the terrain the tubing runs over is hilly. Pressure-compensating emitter tubing typically operates in the range of 10 to 50 psi.

Pressure regulators. Generally there should be a pressure regulator on any drip system since typical household pressure can range from 50 to 100 psi. An exception would be if you were using pressure-compensating emitters and the pressure coming into the system was less than 50 psi, in which case the pressure regulator could be left off. Most standard drip system components operate best between 20 and 40 pounds of pressure, so a good default pressure regulator would be 30 psi. Sprayers and minisprinklers are most affected by changes in pressure. Look for information on adjustable sprayers, sprayers, and sprinklers for specific recommendations. Suppliers offer pressure gauges and pressure regulators to deal with specific situations.

Soil. With drip irrigation, the density of the soil affects how far the water flows from the emitter. Light, sandy soils require a higher rate of water application. Heavy clay and clay loams often benefit from a lower water application rate.

For heavy clay soil, low-flow emitters are recommended. If a high-flow emitter is used, it may exceed the soil's ability to absorb

water, resulting in runoff. Medium-textured soil, on the other hand, requires closer emitter spacing (compared to clay soil). Medium-flow emitters are recommended. Lastly, light-textured soil requires closer emitter spacing in order to uniformly wet the soil profile. High-frequency irrigation can be used to achieve similar results.

Supply. This is a nonstandard use of the term, but I'm using it to indicate how you connect to the water system. This is often a faucet with standard hose threads or a PVC system with pipe from ½ inch to 2 inches or more and threading that may be male, female, or slip (no threads).

Timers. Timers are used to automate your system so that you can water while you're away at work, sleeping, or even out of town. They also ensure that watering will be done on a regular basis. On clay soil or a hillside, short cycles repeated frequently work best. This prevents runoff, erosion, and wasted water. Timers help prevent the too-dry, too-wet cycles that stress plants and retard their growth. They also allow for watering at optimum times, such as early morning or late evening.

Drip irrigation suppliers have windup timers, battery-operated timers, and electronic (multivalve) timers. Windup timers allow you to run water for a certain period and will turn off automatically. They're great for people who forget to turn off their water, but they won't turn on automatically when you're on vacation. Battery-operated timers are simple to install and allow you to program when and how long your system will run. Most of these can even be set for multiple start times per day. Electronic timers are the most reliable, but they can be overkill for systems with fewer than three zones. All timers should be protected from freezing during the winter.

Valve. In drip irrigation there are two types of valves: Manual valves offer great flexibility and control of your irrigation. They can be used in place of automatic valves or within automated systems to shut off areas of your system from irrigation. Automatic valves are used with an electric controller or within a battery timer to automate the watering with your system.

Water pressure (psi). Water pressure describes the force behind the water in a line and is expressed in pounds per square inch (psi). In drip systems, the pressure is commonly limited to 30 psi with a pressure regulator. With non–pressure compensating emitters and sprayers, the higher the pressure, the more water will be put out in a given period of time. See also **pressure (psi).**

Water source. The water source is where the water comes from. This can be a municipal system, a well, a pond, an irrigation ditch, a barrel, or wherever your water comes from. Usually city and well water are easy to filter for drip irrigation systems. Pond, ditch, and some well water have special filtering needs. The quality of the water source will dictate the type of filter necessary for your system. Sand, silt, minerals, organic matter, and rust bacteria are specific concerns. In some cases magnetic water conditioning may be helpful.

Zone. See **hydro zone.**

Note: The preceding glossary of terms and other editorial assistance were supplied by Dripworksusa.com.

8 The Joys of Composting

WOULD YOU DESCRIBE YOURSELF as being pretty gung ho on going green? That's good, because this chapter will teach you the epitome of green: composting. For those of you who've never engaged in composting, you'll find that this chapter answers most questions relating to the "why" of composting (the scientific process of organic decomposition into resulting nutrients) and the "how" (the techniques used or involved in this process).

If you purchased or borrowed this book, you're not likely planning an in-ground garden, so you may think that knowing how to amend—or fertilize—soil won't be a concern. However, as discussed in chapter 6, the health of any garden, whether in the ground or in containers and raised beds, depends upon replenishment of nutrients at some point. And unless you want to spend a fortune on various soil amendments and commercially produced fertilizers, learning how to make your own compost is essential.

So let's get started.

Why Compost?

It's not too difficult to recognize the lack of soil nutrients. Have you ever looked at a field, vacant lot, or other unused plot of land and noted its nearly lifeless, depleted state? It very likely looked dull, dry, or a muddy mess, and as though nothing would grow, much less thrive, in it. In order to grow plants in such soil, it must be amended by good organic matter.

Even if you start your containers and straw-bale gardens with an excellent soil mix, at regular intervals you'll need to rejuvenate it with some fertilizer. The best form of that is natural organic matter. Sure, you can buy commercially produced granulated fertilizers and/or water-soluble types such as Miracle-Gro and others. Various composted materials such as steer manure, peat moss, mushroom compost, and the like are also available for purchase. All of these are great, but most aren't inexpensive. Why not create and use your own free compost by recycling your organic waste at home?

If you look closely around the landscape, you'll realize that nothing is really thrown away in nature. This fact harkens back to the old matter-can-neither-be-created-nor-destroyed rule we all learned in junior high science. Instead, everything is transformed into yet another form, which also happens to be useful to gardeners. So when you engage in any of the various methods of composting, you're taking part in one of the most basic biological cycles of nature: growth and decay.

Composting creates an ideal situation for cleanly transforming raw materials—by the microorganisms, mites, worms, fungi, insects, and other creatures that work on them—to reduce those materials to a rich, fine black humus. These toilers in the soil convert carbon from dead plants into energy, releasing carbon dioxide into the air. In a similar fashion, these soil inhabitants also recycle nutrients from decaying plants into their own bodies and, eventually, back into the soil. As part of this process, other plants and microorganisms use the nutrients and carbon that is released by the composting process. In a circular fashion, the cycle begins again. Some might refer to the resulting compost as substitute manure, since it's so rich and effective in building soil health out of materials that are going to rot anyway.

Speaking of things that are going to rot, did you know that yard waste and vegetable scraps often make up at least 20 percent of household garbage? You can become truly green when you recycle this planet's natural bounty by naturally composting it. It's a much better alternative to sending that stuff to a landfill, where it will add to the Earth's problems by creating methane gas.

Think of it as making life out of leftovers—food for plants! It's similar to naturally occurring soil organic matter in that it holds water and nutrients in the soil. It also makes the soil more porous and much easier to dig or stir up. When you scavenge, save, or hoard things in a composting device—such as coffee grounds, tea or tea bags, eggshells, apple peels, potato skins, wilted lettuce, and other trimmings from fresh produce—you're helping that recycling process. Grass clippings, twigs, leaves, straw, newspapers, paper coffee filters—all these and more are also forms of organic matter that will compost nicely via a natural heating process and decompose directly into the soil. Everything but fat, meat, and dairy can be composted.

> **You can become truly green when you recycle this planet's natural bounty by naturally composting it**

Here's a little scientific trivia: Did you know that the main base for penicillin originally came from a modest little cantaloupe that was found rotting in a grocery store? It sort of created nature's first pharmacy! Bacteria and molds thrive on rotting fruit, and all modern penicillin comes from penicillin mold.

Special Considerations

HEALTH

Be aware that, while composted steer or sterile bovine manure is safe to use in gardens producing edibles, excrement from domestic animals, including cats and dogs, is a no-no. Think of the many diseases, worms, fleas, and other parasites that we treat or try to prevent in our house pets. These can be passed on to humans, and so we must keep their waste out of our gardens.

In recent years, there have been many national and international incidents of serious illness resulting from contaminants in soil. These contaminants, as well as improper food handling, cause food-borne illness. That is a very good reason for minding

Figure 8.1. A commercially made composting bin tucks away unobtrusively yet is easily accessible.   SIDDHARTH PATIL/ WIKIMEDIA COMMONS

what we put into our compost systems. Remember the old computer data axiom, "garbage in, garbage out"? The same principle applies here.

Are there any other health considerations associated with composting? The answer is yes, with the caveat that they're pretty limited. Also, they would only affect the person(s) directly handling and turning the composting materials. People living next door or even casually walking by wouldn't be close enough to be affected.

Few human pathogenic organisms are found in vegetative wastes, but following normal sanitary procedures is important. This is as simple as washing your hands after working with compost and before touching food, your eyes, etc. The majority of people aren't likely to have problems, but a few individuals could be particularly sensitive to some of the organisms in compost. Various molds and fungi found in an active compost process can actually cause allergic responses in some people. Some conditions predisposing individuals to infections or an allergic response would include a weakened immune system, allergies, and asthma.

Also, taking some medications, such as antibiotics and adrenal cortical hormones, or having a punctured eardrum, could be of concern. People with these conditions should avoid turning compost piles or at least take precautions to minimize exposure. Simply wearing common, OSHA-approved dust masks under dry and dusty conditions can effectively minimize potential risks. But, if despite these precautions, individuals still develop an infection or have an allergic reaction to compost, consulting a medical professional is strongly advised.

NEIGHBORS

Let's say you have no health issues and will keep those who do away from your composting area. Before you jump into the composting project, take a brief moment to assess your relationship with your neighbors. If they are avid gardeners who are already

into composting, you know that there'll be no problem of skepticism or opposition from them. It may be, however, that they use only commercially prepared fertilizers and eschew the entire composting shtick. They might erroneously believe that composting inevitably attracts rats, snakes, dogs, cats, raccoons, and other critters. If so, you may need to take a different approach, particularly if you choose to create a simple compost pile right out on the ground.

Here's where you can take a page from a beekeeper's standard practice of gifting neighbors with plenty of honey, wherein the neighbors are kept happy and don't gripe about the bees. In your case, promptly invite the neighbors over to see where you're putting your composting materials and show them that you are covering the decomposing "garbage" with soil. (This particular step is a must and is discussed more later on in this chapter.) Assure them that no fat, meat, or dairy products are composted, which minimizes attracting animals. Point out, too, that you bury bovine or other manure with wood chips, sawdust, and more soil so it won't create an aroma that wafts onto their property. You can even explain how fast the bacterial action proceeds when the pile has enough oxygen to heat up. Show them how completely the scraps, weeds, lawn trimmings, and wood chips are converted to clean, black humus.

Then—ta-da!—when you've grown lots of fresh, healthy vegetables and herbs all fertilized by your composting efforts, you will (yes, you will!) share them with those neighbors. This should be pleasing to them and satisfy their questions, and, hey—who knows? Your enthusiasm could be contagious, and they just might get into composting for themselves!

Overall, the neater and more controlled you make your compost heap seem, and the more you disguise it, the easier your life will be. You can even train decorative vining plants to bedeck the bin or fence. An alternative is a neat, attractive, commercially produced compost bin, which are readily found in garden centers, seed companies' catalogs, and nurseries. These will contain the decaying materials and keep them out of sight. Your options are many, limited only by your own creativity.

The Nuts and Bolts of Composting

Let's get into the nitty-gritty! Why and how does composting actually work? Using organic matter created by composting in your garden is effective because it helps soil particles bind together into aggregates, or clumps. This makes it easy to dig or penetrate. This quality is called tilth. Adding organic matter helps all poor soils, whether they're too sandy or contain too much clay. Soil with good tilth also has good nutrient- and water-holding ability. (Have you ever tried to evenly water an area of soil with heavy clay composition? When it's dried out, it cakes, cracks, and the water either pools up or runs right off. It's an exercise in futility!)

Figure 8.2. The most basic compost pile starts right on the ground.
STEN PORSE/ WIKIMEDIA COMMONS

Even if you do choose to use my methods and get everything up off the ground, you're still going to need to periodically replenish the nutrients in your soil. (An exception is if you use soilless mixes, which is a whole different technique and isn't something that appeals to everyone.) Organic matter improves soil by stimulating or feeding its life. This happens as it provides nutrients to earthworms, bacteria, fungi, and other naturally occurring organisms in the soil. In turn, this recycles the nutrients into forms that are readily available for plants to absorb through their roots. The organic matter also helps to prevent soil and wind erosion; sandy soil particles are bound together and don't disperse so easily.

I should also point out that there are two basic forms of composting: hot and cold. The hot composting method manipulates the decay process, which causes it to proceed quickly. In order to favor the growth of thermophilic (heat-loving) organisms, you must balance food, water, and air in the compost pile or bin. You've heard how heat is generated in compost; when conditions are favorable to high-temperature organisms, a compost pile can quickly heat up to 120°F to 150°F. These high temperatures kill most weed seeds and pathogens (disease organisms), but they don't kill beneficial fungi that help plants' roots absorb nutrition. After the hot phase has been completed, lower-temperature microorganisms, worms, insects, and other invertebrates will complete the decay process.

If you don't have the time to tend a hot compost pile, then you may wish to employ cold composting to turn yard wastes into a usable soil amendment. To do this, you'll simply mix nonwoody yard wastes into a pile and let them sit for a year or so. Even if you use a cold composting process, microorganisms still break down wastes. However, decay is slower, cooler, and not as effective at killing pathogens and weed seeds. Fresh wastes can be added by opening the pile, placing the wastes in the center, and covering them. If you choose to include fruit and vegetable wastes within this pile, you *must* bury them. Should pests prove to be a problem, you may need to screen the pile or choose another method of composting these wastes, as described later in this chapter.

The Components of Compost

Compost components can best be divided into three groups: energy materials, bulking agents, and balanced raw material. First, energy materials provide nitrogen and high-energy carbon compounds; these are needed for fast microbial growth. Second, porous, dry bulking agents help aerate the compost pile. Finally, balanced raw material composts readily without being blended with other ingredients; it has both energy and bulking agent properties. See table 8.1 for some common materials used in making compost.

Table 8.1. Raw materials for compost

Energy sources (high moisture, low porosity, high nitrogen)	Bulking agents (low moisture, high porosity, low nitrogen)	Balanced raw materials (low to medium moisture, medium porosity)
Fresh dairy, chicken, or rabbit manure	Cornstalks	Deciduous leaves
Fruit and vegetable waste	Grass hay	Ground-up shrub and tree trimmings
Garden trimmings	Sawdust	Horse manure and bedding
Grass clippings	Wheat straw	Legume hay
	Wood chips	

Obviously, the right balance of moisture, air, and nutrients for achieving rapid composting can be had by mixing bulking agents with energy sources. A mixture comprised of one part energy source with two parts bulking agent (by volume) will usually give an acceptable mix for rapid composting. Smaller particles are

easier to mix, and they have more surface area for microbial activity. Chopping, grinding, cutting, or smashing raw materials reduces particle size.

Extensive research and testing has taught us that soil must have an adequate balance of nutrients. I never took a chemistry class in high school or college and don't need to present one here. (There'll be no test at the end of this chapter, either!) We'll just take a look at the basics.

Knowing how and why these nutrients work will help you succeed in your composting efforts.

Knowing how and why these nutrients work will help you succeed in your composting efforts. It will also aid you later on in diagnosing and differentiating plant diseases versus soil nutrient deficiency symptoms in your plants.

The three nutrients we concentrate on the most in garden soil are: nitrogen, phosphorus, and potassium (NPK). (These were mentioned in chapter 6 in the discussion of soils.) You may hear other gardeners tossing around these terms and words, and talking about the excess or dearth of these nutrients in their own plants. Let's explore each of these nutrients and why each is so important, as well as micronutrients.

Nitrogen, known as capital N, is the biggie here; it has a major effect on the growth and yield of crop plants. It always gets the most emphasis in soil analysis because, after carbon, oxygen, and hydrogen, it's required by plants in the greatest amounts—plant proteins are 16 percent nitrogen. It's found only in the organic fraction of soils and is easily leached in the nitrate form. Annual plants need nitrogen the most at about three to four weeks after seedlings have emerged or after transplanting.

While nitrogen can be taken up by the plants, it can also be lost to leaching, runoff, erosion, and escape from the soil surface into the atmosphere by volatilization, depending on its form. Nitrogen exists in the soil in organic and inorganic forms. It's continually transformed through biological and chemical reactions; these processes constitute the nitrogen cycle. You can see the dichotomy: Too little nitrogen results in unhealthy plants, and too much nitrogen can create problems. Most notably (your attention, please!), it can be a source of groundwater pollution. This is why we're urged not to "feed" lawns to prevent weeds; the runoff of all that nitrogen creates big problems down the line in creeks, rivers, lakes, etc. Just as everything in "Goldilocks and the Three Bears" had to measure up, the nitrogen balance needs to be "just right."

In its gaseous form, nitrogen is useless to plants. However, certain free-living bacteria (e.g., microbes such as rhizobium) living in nodules on the roots of legumes (peas, beans, etc.) can convert atmospheric nitrogen into plant-available forms. The free-living nitrogen fixers in this world all rely on the same enzyme, nitrogenase, to do the job. (Interestingly, our planet's entire supply of nitrogenase could fit into a single large bucket, even though all of the nitrogen contained within proteins and genes of plants—as well as animals, including humans—at one time or another has been funneled through these nitrogen-fixing microbes.) If you live near farming areas, you may have noticed that fields usually planted in corn or other nutrient-demanding crops are often rested for a year. A nitrogen-rich legume crop, such as vetch, is grown instead to replenish and renourish worn-out soil. Then it gets plowed back into the soil the following season prior to planting a regular food crop.

When highly carbonaceous materials such as straw, wood chips, and sawdust are incorporated into the soil, it can be robbed of nitrogen and become immobilized. Because soil microbes require nitrogen in order to digest organic matter, they will convert plant-available inorganic forms of nitrogen to organic forms: proteins. Since soil microbes eat first at the "nutrient table," this can

cause a nitrogen deficiency in your garden, resulting in puny, piti-ful, less-than-robust plants. The nitrogen then hangs around doing nothing, immobilized in the microbes until they die and de-compose.

Immobilization may also be caused by manure with large amounts of undecomposed bedding (straw, etc.), so you must add about 1 to 1½ pounds of nitrogen for each 100 dry pounds of these low-nitrogen materials. Fresh green wastes, such as grass clippings, are higher in nitrogen than dry materials. This is where you need to pay attention and not dump this stuff just anywhere, expecting it to decompose effectively on its own.

Mineralization deserves mention here; it's the conversion of organic nitrogen from plant and animal remains to inorganic im-modium. This is then either held by soil colloids, is used by plants, or is transformed in nitrate nitrogen. Then we have nitrification. What the heck is that? It's the conversion by soil microbes of am-monium to *nitrite* nitrogen and then to *nitrate* nitrogen. The process is accelerated when your soil is warm, moist, and well aerated—a lovely environment for growing plants.

Finally, we must consider denitrification, the process that oc-curs in poorly drained soils when nitrates are converted by bac-teria to nitrogen gas, which then escapes into the atmosphere. It's the opposite, obviously, of nitrification. Ammonia gas can also be lost to the atmosphere when manure is dropped on the garden and not incorporated; that results in volatilization.

Now let's take a peek at phosphorus, abbreviated in gardening "chemistry" as capital *P*. Phosphorus is very important in many of the biochemical functions needed to have a healthy plant. Phosphate compounds are involved in making and storing energy in the plant. This nutrient is found at plant growth centers (root tips and shoots), so overall plant growth suffers when P is defi-cient. Phosphorus is especially critical at establishment. Availabil-ity in the soil is affected by pH. (The pH scale measures how acidic or alkaline a substance is and ranges from 0 to 14; 7 is neutral.) At a pH lower than 6, phosphorus is tied up in forms that are not available to plants.

Potassium, abbreviated as capital K, helps to regulate the enzyme activity in plants, facilitates carbohydrate production and transport, and regulates water content in cells and water loss from stomates on leaves. It's needed to help improve the plant's tolerance to drought, high and low temperatures, and wear stress.

Last but not least are micronutrients. These minor elements are essential for good plant growth but are required in very small quantities. Micronutrients include sulfur, calcium, magnesium, manganese, copper, zinc, iron, boron, molybdenum, chlorine, cobalt, and nickel. Micronutrient availability in the soil is highly dependent on pH and the presence of other nutrient ions. An excess of one element may show up as a deficiency of another.

So now you know what's so great about composting and why we need to amend soil in order to foster healthy growth in plants! But where do we use organic matter such as compost? Anywhere you can, as often as you can! One of the most important things homeowners can do is amend the soil of planting areas for landscaping. Trees, shrubs, lawns, and herbaceous plants all benefit, as do vegetable gardens, fruit orchards, and other areas under cultivation.

When in doubt, carefully examine your plants to see if there are excess symptoms or deficiency occurrence and disease. With a little practice, you will soon learn to differentiate between them and possible disease or insect damage. This will help you recognize that something is missing or, conversely, present in excess. You can then take corrective measures. Also see chapter 10 on diseases for more help with puzzling symptoms.

Rebuilding the Soil

Naturally, if you're already consuming organically produced food (grown via sustainable gardening practices and without synthetic pesticides or fertilizers), you can be assured that your compost is as organic as possible. The resulting material can then be used in place of or in addition to a commercial fertilizer preparation. Table 8.2 lists organic and inorganic sources of fertilizer, along with the nitrogen (N), phosphorus (P), and potassium (K) control of each material. This will enable you to see the advantages and availability of these three nutrients in materials commonly available to add to the soil.

Other kinds of organic matter come from all over the country's lakes, orchards, vineyards, and fields. Fruit pomace (seeds, pulp, skin); seaweed; brewery waste; buckwheat hulls; fish industry as well as mushroom waste; and zoo, fair, and circus waste may be available in specific regions. Paper products, too, should not be overlooked, as several of them—especially newspaper and cardboard—are quite useful in the garden, particularly when composted properly. Although paper doesn't provide nutrients, it is organic material composed primarily of wood fibers. Used in a compost pile, it provides structure while decomposing slowly.

Good choices include shredded newspaper or telephone book paper; they can be composted or dug into soil directly. They decompose nicely when mixed with high nitrogen products, such as a manure. Shredded newspaper also works with other mulches in the landscape, where earthworms break it down. Although it breaks down slowly, shredded computer or other office paper can also be used. It is wise, however, not to use glossy magazine-style paper, as it contains dioxins, which creates concerns. Also, forget about waxed paper; it almost never breaks down.

Finally, table 8.3 gives a brief comparison of just using peat

Table 8.2. Mineral nutrient value of organic material

Material	Nitrogen (% N)	Phosphorous (% P205)	Potassium (% K20)	Relative nutrient availability
Wood ashes (may raise pH)	0	1–2	3–7	Rapid
Urea	42–45	0	0	Rapid
Sewage sludge (digested)	1–3	0.5–4	0–0.5	Slow
Sawdust	4	2	4	Very slow
Peat and muck	1.5–3	0.25–0.5	0.5–1	Very slow
Mushroom compost	0.4–0.7	1–2	0.5–1.5	Slow
Milorganite (dry)	5	2–5	2	Medium
Swine manure	0.3	0.3	0.3	Medium
Poultry manure (50% water)	2	2	1	Medium rapid
Sheep manure	0.3	0.15	0.5	Medium
Cattle manure	0.25	0.15	0.25	Medium
Horse manure	0.3	0.15	0.5	Medium
Fish meal (dry)	10	4	0	Slow
Dried blood (dry)	12	1.5	0.57	Medium rapid
Cottonseed meal (dry)	6	2.5	1.7	Slow medium
Compost (not fortified)	1.5–3.5	0.5–1	1–2	Slow
Cocoa shell meal	2.5	1	2.5	Slow
Bonemeal (steamed)	0.7–4	10–34	0	Slow medium
Bonemeal (raw)	2–6	15–27	0	Slow

moss, a popular commercially produced composting product, versus using a natural home-produced compost. Pretty telling, isn't it?

Table 8.3. Peat moss versus home-produced compost

Peat moss	Compost
Inexpensive	Often free
Poor in nutrients	Relatively rich in nutrients, but not a fertilizer
Low pH	Usually neutral or slightly alkaline pH
Doesn't compact	May compact
Excellent water-holding ability	Good at holding water
Difficult to rewet	Rewetting capacity varies
Uniform composition	Variable in composition and contaminants
Possibility of pathogens	Full of mostly beneficial microorganisms
No weed seed content	May have weed seeds if not composted properly*
Little to no disease-suppressing qualities	Able to suppress some plant disease pathogens
Uses a natural resource	Recycles organic waste matter
Not usable for mulch	Excellent as a mulch

*This refers to cases where the compost either goes anaerobic, hasn't heated up enough for an adequate period of time, or hasn't been sufficiently turned to expose all particles to hot temperatures. These factors are all crucial for the destruction of weed seeds.

Methods of Accumulating Composting Materials

There are many ways to compost wastes. The method of composting you choose will depend on whether you plan to compost yard and garden wastes or kitchen wastes (or both), how much money and time you wish to spend, how much space you have, and how soon you need the compost. Take a look at table 8.4, which compares the decomposition time and cost of various types of composting systems. This will help you to plan.

Table 8.4. Composting systems compared by cost and decomposition time

System used	Cost	Time for finished compost (rate of composting yard waste)
Compost mound	None	Slow if not turned; fast if turned often
Holding unit	Low	Slow
Turning unit	High	Fast; minimum 6 weeks
Mulch	Low	Can use immediately, but material should be shredded
Commercial bin	High	Fast; minimum 2 weeks
Kitchen waste	None	Can use immediately
Compost pockets	Low	Slow; faster if turned or mixed
Garbage can composter	Medium	Fast; minimum 4 weeks
Worm composting bin	High	Fast; minimum 6 weeks

Now it's time to look at your options for starting the composting process. Note that in addition to the containers described in this chapter, there are other options, including turning units and commercially produced bins. It all depends on what will work for you.

Compost Mounds

The most common way to compost yard wastes without a bin is in a simple, uncontained mound (see fig. 8.4, *top*). The only costs for this method will be your time and work. All you'll need is a shovel or a pitchfork and work gloves.

Find a good location and pile your yard waste into a mound, say about 3 feet × 3 feet × 3 feet. This pile should be covered with a layer of soil to keep in moisture. This helps the microorganisms and soil animals that work to make compost.

As waste become available, add them to the pile. This includes nonwood materials such as garden waste and grass clippings; they

Figure 8.3. Here's a single pile of compost, and then a two-pile system.

work best. Remember the discussion of hot and cold composting earlier in the chapter? Those methods differentiate between compost being ready earlier versus later. You'll have to make the decision about which way you want to go, at least at the start. You may find, over time, that one method works better for your lifestyle than the other, and you can modify it later on.

To ideally maintain a compost pile, it's best to have two piles, if you have the space and interest (see fig. 8.3, *bottom*). Once the first pile is large enough, stop adding any organic material and let it go to work. Meanwhile, start the second pile. It's important to keep the pile(s) moist but not soaked—all the more so if it isn't covered with soil. This is where you can speed up the composting process (hot composting) by turning the pile. Your home-created compost should be ready in three to four months, or in one year if you don't turn the pile.

Compost Bins Made of Wire Mesh or Hardware Cloth

For a step up, try making a wire mesh bin (see fig. 8.4, *left*). It's inexpensive and easy to build. Use either galvanized chicken wire or hardware cloth (nongalvanized chicken wire can be used, but it won't last very long). Posts, such as 3-foot wooden plant stakes, provide ideal stability for a chicken wire bin. I set mine directly onto a fastened-down section of the Typar weed barrier since rodents cannot penetrate it from above or below. Turning the compost with a pitchfork is easily accomplished with this bin.

To make a wire mesh bin, you'll need the following materials:

- 12½ feet of 36-inch wide, 1-inch galvanized chicken wire or ½-inch hardware cloth
- heavy wire or plastic ties
- 3 or 4 wooden or metal posts (for chicken wire bin)

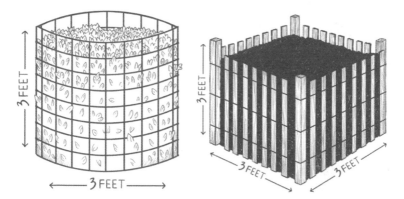

Figure 8.4. A simple chicken-wire bin works well, and the snow-fencing model is also easy to use.

You'll also need the following tools:

- heavy-duty wire or tin snips
- pliers
- hammer (for chicken wire bin)
- metal file (for hardware cloth bin)
- work gloves

Now you're ready. If you're building the bin with chicken wire, do the following:

1. Fold back 3 to 4 inches of wire at each end of the cut piece to provide a strong, clean edge that won't poke or snag and will latch easily.
2. Stand the wire in a circle and set in place for the compost pile.
3. Cut the heavy wire into lengths for ties, or set out sufficient plastic ties. Attach the ends of the chicken wire together, using either wire ties (use pliers) or plastic ties.
4. Space wood or metal posts around the inside of the (chicken) wire circle. Hold the posts tightly against the wire, and pound them firmly into the ground to provide support. They can go directly through the weed barrier, if you're using it.

If you're building the bin using hardware cloth (same principle as fig. 8.4, *left*), then do the following:

1. Trim the ends of the hardware cloth so the wires are flush with a cross wire. You're doing this to get rid of sharp edges that could poke or scratch hands. Lightly file each wire along the cut edge to ensure safe handling when opening or closing the bin. (Or you could meticulously snip off any sharp protruding wires.)

2. Bend the hardware cloth into a circle and stand it in place for the compost pile.

3. Cut the heavy wire into lengths for ties, or use plastic ties. Attach the ends of the hardware cloth together. (Use pliers if using wire ties.) Pound in support stakes or posts as described for the wire bin.

Go ahead and add wastes as they become available. As with the uncontained mound, nonwood materials such as grass clippings and garden weeds work very well. The decomposing process can be speeded up by chopping or shredding the wastes.

Let's suppose now that you have created two open piles or bins. The material at the bottom will become compost sooner than the material at the top, as you keep adding wastes. If using a wire bin with support posts, you'll need to open the bin where you attached the ends together. Use a pitchfork or shovel to remove the compost from the top of one of the piles or bins and place it on top of the second pile or bin. Then you can scoop out the material at the bottom of the first pile or bin and use it in your garden.

Close up the wire bin and/or return the wire bin to its original spot. Either use the pitchfork to put some of the top of the second pile's contents into the emptied one, or just add material as it accumulates.

Other Composting Devices

Now let's look at some other options for composting devices.

Snow fencing (see fig. 8.4, *right*). Wrap a 12½-foot length of 36-inch-high (minimum) fencing into a square. Pound posts into four corners for support.

Cinder blocks (see fig. 8.5). If you wish to make this bin, you'll need about 26 cinder blocks (optional: about 32 blocks for a second bin), and don't forget the work gloves. You will be constructing a three-sided bin here.

1. Place five cinder blocks in a row along the ground at your composting site. Be sure to leave about a ½-inch space below each block to let in air.

2. Place four cinder blocks in another row along the ground perpendicular to and at one end of the first row, forming a

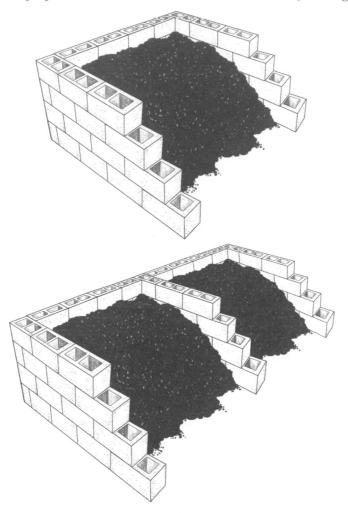

Figure 8.5. Here we have the concrete bin, in a single compartment, and then in a two-bin system. Both are simple to construct.

square corner. Again, be sure to leave about a ½-inch space between each block.

3. In the same way, place four blocks at the opposite end of the first row. This forms a three-sided enclosure, the same as you'll see at garden centers and other establishments that supply soil amendments (such as mulches, bark dust, various composts, and so forth) in bulk quantities.

4. Add a second layer of blocks, staggering them to increase stability, again leaving about a ½ inch between each block. There is no need to use mortar or cement, so don't do it!

5. Add a third layer of blocks, again staggering them to increase stability. There should be five blocks across the back of the enclosure and three on each side.

6. The last and top layer should have four blocks across the back and three on each side.

7. Optional: To decrease composting time, you can build a second bin next to the first. That way, the wastes in one bin will mature while you add wastes to the other. If you build two bins, use one side wall of the first bin as a common wall so you only need to build two additional walls. (See fig. 8.5, *bottom.*)

As with the other composting methods, add wastes as they become available. Remember that grass clippings and garden weeds (nonwood materials) work best. Chop or shred them for faster decomposition.

Compost Bins Made of Wood

Finally, you have the option of building a wooden box bin. This can be built quite inexpensively by using wooden pallets (referred to in some areas as "skids"). These are often available from manufacturers and landfills. A nicer looking bin can be made with new lumber; it's up to your personal taste and neighborhood standards.

To make a wooden box bin out of pallets (see fig. 8.6), you'll need the following materials:

- 4 wooden pallets (5 if you want a bottom in the container) sized to make a four-sided container at least 3 feet × 3 feet × 3 feet
- nails, wire, or plastic ties

To make the bin, complete the following:

1. Nail or wire four pallets together to make a four-sided container at least 3 feet square.

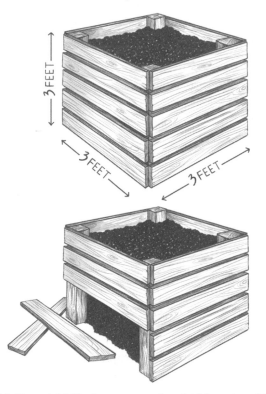

Figure 8.6. You might like to use a wooden-slat bin system. The second example sports removable slats at the bottom for easy access to the finished compost.

2. You're done! The container is ready to use.

As indicated in the materials list, you can add a fifth pallet on the bottom to use as a base. Doing this will allow more air to get into the pile, which helps the composting process and also increases the bin's stability.

To build a bin out of lumber, you'll need the following:

- 1 12-foot length of 2 × 4 lumber
- 5 12-foot lengths of 6 × ¾ lumber nails

How to assemble:

1. Saw the 12-foot length of 2 × 4 lumber into four pieces, each 3 feet long. These will be used as corner posts.
2. Choose a (preferably level) 3-foot-square site for your compost bin. Pound the four posts into the ground 3 feet apart, at the corners of the square.
3. Saw each of the five 12-foot boards into four 3-foot pieces. Starting at the bottom, you will nail the boards to the posts to make a four-sided container, allowing five boards to a side. Be sure to leave a ½ inch between the boards to allow air to get into the pile.

If you're handy with carpentry, you may want to make the bottom two or three horizontal slats removable. Then when you're ready to remove the finished compost at the bottom, you will simply remove those slats and lift the composted material out. Replace the slats when you're finished, and add new wastes when they are available. (See fig. 8.6.) You can also choose to build a second holding unit (which will share its inside wall with the first bin) to decrease your composting time. While waiting for the wastes in one to mature, you can add wastes to the other.

Personally, I like to separate my organic waste materials designated for composting into two categories: green waste (energy

materials) and brown waste (bulking agents). Green waste consists of vegetable and fruit trimmings, eggshells, coffee grounds (and paper filters), and other items that are connected to our edibles. These are first collected in the kitchen, and any covered container will do: plastic, crockery, stainless steel, etc. There are many products available made to sit discreetly on a countertop; simply place your discards into this receptacle and periodically empty it into your compost system. Composting green waste works best if you coarsely chop up any large pieces of fruits or vegetables (onions, cucumbers, apples, melon rinds, etc.) first, as it helps them break down more rapidly.

Figure 8.7. Another composting bin uses a plastic container placed into a metal garbage can. Then the whole thing is set into a hole in the ground at a depth suitable for easy turning and removal.

DIEGO GREZ/ WIKIMEDIA COMMONS

Outside in my garden space, I use a commercial black compost bin with a trap in the bottom for removing the finished compost created by this green waste. This unit prevents problems with critters helping themselves and making a mess. And it's out of sight and nonodorous to any visitors or guests. At the time of this writing I had just purchased a rotating/turning bin, so it will be another year before I know how well it works.

Brown waste, on the other hand, is yard trimmings, grass clippings, leaves, twigs, tree cones, and other items. I put these items into my open chicken-wire bins, out in the air, where there's not much reason for interference by birds or animals. However, having said that, you will probably want to keep a lookout for burrowing critters and discourage their presence during the gardening season. Who cares if they temporarily move in for the winter? They can be chased out when winter is on the wane.

Important reminder one more time: *Never* add meat, pet food (dry or wet) and other animal products, and dairy products to the pile! Make sure that everyone else in your household fully understands this rule and the reasons for it: It impedes the decomposition process, creates odors, and attracts animals.

Turning Composting Material

No matter which composting method you use, you'll need to turn the compost at least weekly. Remember to put a layer of soil on top and to keep the compost moist but not soaked. As shown in table 8.4, the length of time it takes for the compost to break down and become usable varies.

To turn the pile, simply slip the tines of a pitchfork (not a garden spade) underneath the top few inches. Lift it up and place it to the side momentarily. Use either the pitchfork or a shovel to scoop up and turn over the bottom layers, then replace the top layer, making sure to fluff it and turn it over as you do so.

If you don't turn the pile every week or so, you may find that the materials aren't decomposing very quickly. This may create odors, or the pile may stay too wet. Table 8.5 should help you diagnose any problematic conditions in the piles or bins.

Table 8.5. Composting problems and solutions

Symptom	Problem	How to fix it
Pile is wet and smells like a mixture of rancid butter, vinegar, and rotten eggs	Not enough air, too much nitrogen, or too wet	(1) Turn pile (2) Add straw, sawdust, or wood chips (3) Provide drainage
Pile doesn't heat up	Pile is too small or too dry	(1) Make pile larger (2) Add water
Pile is damp and sweet smelling but won't heat up	Not enough nitrogen	Add grass clippings or other sources of nitrogen
Center is dry and contains tough materials	Not enough water	(1) Add water (2) Turn pile
Pile is attracting animals	Meat and other animal products have been added	(1) Keep meat and other animal products out of the pile (2) Enclose pile in ¼-inch hardware cloth

Using Compost in Your Plantings

When some finished compost is ready and you need to fertilize your plants and rejuvenate your soil, all you have to do is go to your compost pile or container and scoop out the "black gold" from the bottom. It should be dark and rich, and look as though plants could grow in it at a moment's notice. You'll probably find earthworms happily living in it! Collect a quantity in a container or bucket and, using a small trowel or your hand, work a cupful or so of the compost at a time into your grower's pots and other containers and raised beds, taking care not to disturb or uproot any existing desirable plants. It's not necessary to add a huge amount.

If possible, keep a notebook in which you've set up a fertilization schedule; it will remind you to check your plants' health and give them a periodic "meal." For details on diagnosing specific plant problems or diseases, please see chapter 10.

Well, that's the story of composting. Should you have any unanswered questions or concerns, don't hesitate to consult someone who gardens well or your local extension service, either in person or online.

9 Sustainable Gardening Practices for Weed and Pest Control

BY USING THE OFF-THE-GROUND gardening methods espoused in this book, you will not be plagued by any meaningful quantity of weeds such as those found in traditional, in-ground gardens. Crawling pests will not be able to take over your garden, either. So this chapter will be relatively short.

Chemical versus Natural Pesticides

My own personal dictum regarding weeds and bugs is to follow the principles and practices of organic, sustainable gardening. As we've discussed, organic gardening means the process of building soil without the use of synthetic chemical pesticides and using natural fertilizers rather than synthetic ones. That doesn't mean you can't use natural pesticides and fertilizers—you can and should! As you read this chapter, you'll learn more about that. If you are composting your organic wastes, you'll find that the resulting rich, natural fertilizer will do its share and then some to keep your garden healthy.

In this chapter, I'm focusing on integrated pest management, hereafter referred to as IPM, an ecological approach to pest control. The main factor in IPM is the threshold, or level of tolerance, of a problem or imperfection. That threshold is the point at which you decide you must treat the "problem," which is usually represented by imperfect or damaged leaves, flowers, or produce. Produce can be imperfect yet tasty and healthful, and there isn't a need for most homes to have weed-free turf. While this approach shouldn't be much of a problem to use in your off-the-ground garden, it deserves some attention and a few cautions. You'll note the word *sustainable* in this chapter's title. In the context here, the term means using IPM gardening techniques and methods that stay one jump ahead of plant and insect/animal pests. Your garden can be kept going from season to season without making any risky moves that could compromise it.

> **Produce can be imperfect yet tasty and healthful, and there isn't a need for most homes to have weed-free turf.**

I prefer using these strategies—commonly referred to as "cultural methods"—for pest management; they're easy, simple, and effective. Think of it as being proactive with your green thumb! Using pesticides (the term applied collectively to herbicides and insecticides) becomes unnecessary; your soil and plants will be kept healthy, while any pests and weeds will be kept under control or nonexistent. Desirable plantings and adjacent areas won't be contaminated with harmful chemicals (see fig. 9.1), and—best of all—people and

Figure 9.1. Please leave the nasty chemicals out of the garden!

domestic animals won't be in danger if they come into contact with your soil and plants.

One of the greatest benefits from getting your garden off the ground's surface is that the weeds will be few and far between, and you won't have to dig in the ground to remove them! One simple tug from a comfortable stance, and that little sucker will come right out. By the way, many weeds in your yard and garden, including dandelions, can be killed by simply pouring boiling water or strong vinegar on them. They respond like the Wicked Witch in the *Wizard of Oz* when she whines, "I'm melting, I'm melting!"

The same principle applies to dealing with four-or-more-legged pests. When all plants are either in containers or 3 feet off the ground in a straw-bale raised bed, it's not easy for ground crawlers to hoof it all the way up to the top and find a hospitable

home right there in plain sight. Rabbits can't make the climb; other delicacy-seeking chompers such as red squirrels and chipmunks might try but will be easily exposed (as in "Get off there, you rascal!"). I'm always surprised by the fact that, while wild rabbits frequently hop through our garden area, they have never nibbled so much as one leaf or carrot top from our containers, even though the plants are clearly within munching height. Go figure!

Deer, too, may come around, and there are many methods for keeping them at bay. Depending on your area's population of vegetarians such as deer and rabbits, find out how other local people deal with them in conjunction with a vegetable garden environment. (Check with your extension service if you need assistance.) While some of my master gardener colleagues grimly resort to erecting strong fences around their food production areas, others swear by using mothballs, animal hair, predator urine, and other materials as repellants. A liberal sprinkling of powdered or ground cayenne pepper directly into the containers will usually put a stop to the erstwhile munching.

Chipmunks in particular don't like plants that are sticky, hairy, or strong smelling

Chipmunks in particular don't like plants that are sticky, hairy, or strong smelling. I've learned to mix such plants in with my annual flowers to keep Alvin, Simon, and Theodore out of the posy planters. That, along with the powdered cayenne pepper, usually keeps them and squirrels from bothering the flowers.

Occasionally, the wind will give an assist to some stray weed seeds, which may decide that your containers or raised bed offer perfect hospitality. Of course, the first place to start in weed prevention is to check your garden soil. Examine it before you bring it to your lot, unless you're purchasing commercially bagged, sterile planting mix or potting soil. However, even then problems sometimes occur.

Here's an example. Some friends told me how one time they brought home a few bags of a special growing mix (marketed by a reputable company), intended for rapidly growing prolific plants. When they opened the bags, there were already flowers and weeds growing inside! That company had apparently slipped up on the soil sterilization process; weed and other seeds that should have been killed in the heating process had survived. This isn't good, considering how much that special mix costs—which is another argument of mixing one's own growing mix.

Also watch container plants from nurseries, garden exchanges, or plant sales. A few particularly tough plants, such as oxalis, buttercup, and weedy veronica, may come along with the desired plants. Remove any signs of these sprouting plants before setting containers out into the garden.

One time I tried saving some of the previous year's soil and covered it on a tarp for the winter. The following year, I mixed it in with fresh amendments. Well, what a surprise I had when hundreds of nicotiana plants mysteriously sprouted from that soil, in every container I'd used it in! The confounded things hadn't bloomed the previous year, but there they were in all their glory. (Solution: Sterilize previously used soil before using it.)

Voracious chewing insects that fly around looking for leafy greens will receive short shrift in containers or the high raised beds. If an enterprising bird doesn't spot them first and scarf them down for lunch, you'll spot them when you do periodic inspections or harvesting. Simply pluck them out and dispose of them in either soapy water or by some other final means (like a good stomp!). Ditto with any larvae, cutworms, or other critters that may occasionally try to take up residence.

If your property is close to other neighbors, you might want to cultivate a relationship with them that allows for a coordinated

approach to weeds that hitch a ride on the wind. Dandelions are a good example of this. Yards that have been taken over by that yellow-blooming weed will eventually sprout a kazillion puffballs of seeds that have no compunction about landing in your soil, wherever it may be. If they are expanding their presence in the vicinity of your vegetable garden, try the boiling water method. As mentioned before, it works great for killing dandelions, and frequent use of it throughout the growing season should keep them to a minimum.

Now, having said that, I do make one exception in weed control of tenacious pests, such as bindweed (*Convulvulus arvensis*), elsewhere in the ground of my garden area. This cousin of the common morning glory will absolutely take over if not firmly removed by a combination of hand weeding and applying glyphosate to the roots, usually in the fall. Glyphosate (sold commercially as RoundUp) is the only herbicide I ever use, and then only in a very controlled, judicious application when nothing else works. It's a systemic, nonselective, foliar-applied herbicide; it potentially affects any plant with which it comes into contact. It isn't usually picked up by roots unless they are exposed in some manner. I use a cardboard shield to ensure that the only plant hit with the chemical is the one I want to eliminate. You can read more about glyphosate on any university-based, agricultural, or extension service website or in the product literature found on the bottle. That's all I'm going to say about pesticides, because I generally avoid them like the plague.

Harmful versus Beneficial Garden Visitors

What about pests with six or more legs? Without taking you through a complete course in entomology (the study of insects), it would behoove you to know who's beneficial and who's harmful

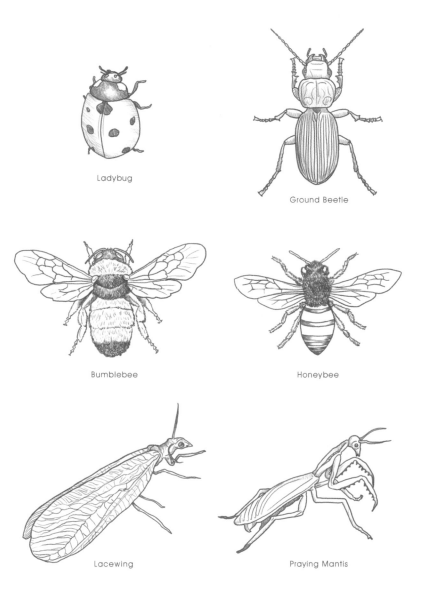

Ladybug

Ground Beetle

Bumblebee

Honeybee

Lacewing

Praying Mantis

Figure 9.2. Here's a lineup of desirable visitors to be welcomed into the garden.

in the garden. Obviously, any of the "good" bees—honeybees, bumblebees, and mason bees—and lady beetles (also called ladybugs) should be welcomed with open arms. So should most wasps, spiders, ground beetles, praying mantis, pirate bugs, and several species of flies. (See fig. 9.2 for some examples of beneficial garden visitors.)

Please don't get hysterical around bees and wasps; never swat at them, as that's very annoying and is almost certain to make them turn nasty and get in a mood to sting you. Just walk away and don't run for the bug spray. We need all of the waste eaters and pollinators we can get! I'm a retired beekeeper, and so I'm admittedly pro-buzzies in the garden. If you are truly allergic to bee stings (i.e., you go into anaphylactic shock when stung), ask your physician to prescribe an EpiPen for you to carry, and be sure you know how to use it.

The rule here is: Know your garden buddies as well as the enemies, and avoid killing them inadvertently. Insecticides have no place in a vegetable garden unless you have an out-of-control infestation—and that won't happen when you garden off the ground, unless you're really negligent. Even then, you can still use sanitary and cultural control techniques to attack the problem before resorting to "better living through chemistry." A soap-and-water mixture in a handheld spray bottle will take care of many pest and disease symptoms on plants.

> **Know your garden buddies as well as the enemies, and avoid killing them inadvertently.**

Japanese beetles, tomato hornworms, squash bugs, cucumber beetles, flea beetles, ants, cabbage moths, aphids, and borers are not to be offered any hospitality at all. Too, mollusks such as slugs and snails are definitely not welcome. They are easily discouraged

Figure 9.3. Green onions and chives share space with parsley and cilantro.   GREG ASPINALL

Figure 9.4. Plant diversity is good for the garden, besides providing spot color, as these nasturtiums do.   GEORGE CHERNILEVSKY/ WIKIMEDIA COMMONS

and/or controlled by various methods in aboveground gardens, including picking them off by hand and dropping them into soapy water. (Wearing gloves is a good idea when doing this.) Another option is to put out a 1-inch-deep jar lid or similar container filled with beer. Set it into a slight low spot in the ground, and it will attract slugs and lead them to a (hic!) beer-soaked death.

An easy, green way to deal with this issue is to make diverse plantings. You can place containers of flowers among your containers of vegetables and herbs—which works great if you have a contingency of hungry chipmunks hanging around. This also works with straw-bale raised beds. Try planting dill, marigolds, chives, onions, parsley, basil, and other strongly scented herbs or flowers throughout the garden area. If you allow parsley, carrots,

Figure 9.5. A Tobacco Hornworm! No one wants these in their garden.
SUPER RAD!/ WIKIMEDIA COMMONS

and celery to remain in place over the winter, they will produce flowers during the second season and attract beneficial insects.

Also, plant strong-smelling herbs among vegetable crops. Basil planted among tomatoes may repel tomato hornworms; a pot of

nasturtiums climbing up the trellis near squash may repel squash bugs. Tomato plants placed next to asparagus may repel asparagus beetles. Try putting marigolds, mints, thyme, or chamomile next to your cabbage plants. When growing squash and cucumbers, radishes make excellent trap crops for cucumber beetles. Observe your plants as they grow, and make note of combinations that seem to work for pest control and growth enhancement. Who knows, you just might be the first person to discover a new set of compatible plants!

Many insects eat or parasitize harmful insects, and they can help your gardening efforts. You can attract these beneficial insects by putting flowering plants near the garden. Dill, parsley, carrot, coriander (cilantro), angelica, and parsnip (the edible

Figure 9.6. Radishes emerge next to green onions and herbs.

GREG ASPINALL

kind), which feature flat-topped clusters of small flowers that have strong fragrances, seem to attract large numbers of beneficial insects, particularly predatory wasps and flies. This makes them excellent candidates for companion planting in your large grower's pots or straw-bale garden.

What makes certain plants suitable for beneficial insects? The pollen or nectar is readily accessible, which is helpful to beneficial insects since they have small mouth parts. They also need a high protein and sugar diet all season, so including some plants that bloom early and continually is helpful. Nectar-rich plants will attract pollinators and other helpful insects.

If you want to deliberately attract a broad, predatory insect population to your garden, you must provide these things: nectar or other insects, water, shelter, and places to breed. If the habitat plants are not fully established in the garden, additional food should be provided

Nectar-rich plants will attract pollinators and other helpful insects.

to keep beneficials around during any lags in the pest population. While commercial products are available, a simple sugar/water mix of one part sugar to four parts water is very attractive if sprayed on lower plant leaves. Lady beetles and lacewings especially like this. It's one of the most effective techniques for attracting or keeping them and establishing any recently purchased beneficials, which are often available in garden centers and good nurseries.

Water is absolutely essential, not only for your plants but also for the beneficial critters who are going to help your garden. It should be available in nearby birdbaths, fountains or other water features, and ponds or streams. Ideally, it will be located within the immediate garden.

For the best results, you'll need to provide two types of locations. First, an elevated dish or shallow birdbath (lined with stones) helps flying insects. There must be a place for them to land and drink, hence the stones. Second, crawling insects need ground-level water dishes. (These are also popular with toads, which eat the bad bugs.) To get maximum benefit, place these water sources every 400 square feet within your protected garden area. You may think that maintaining standing water could encourage mosquito buildup, but an organic garden full of insects is more likely to sport a healthy population of birds, toads, lizards, snakes, or bats, which generally cure the problem of mosquitoes by stirring up the water and eating the flying pests. If you want to attract butterflies, set out a shallow pan of soil and add enough water to create sloppy mud. This is the only mechanism that permits butterflies to take in water. Keep the soil moist at all times.

Figure 9.7. The American toad is an adorable and very welcome garden visitor.   CHRISTINAT3/ WIKIMEDIA COMMONS

Let's take a closer look at those other natural predators.

Toads eat many insects and will remain in the garden if there is water at ground level, along with hiding places. Examples are rock groupings, under boards or brush piles, or "toad houses" made from inverted clay pots with a chipped lip for entry.

The common brown bat can eat 3,000 insects (mosquitoes and flies) in a night! Bat houses, breeding houses, and an accessible water source are good investments.

Birds are attracted to a healthy, organic garden and provide significant pest control. Be sure to provide water and do not spray pesticides (either herbicides for weeds or insecticides for bugs), which sicken or kill many birds. Feeding birds during the summer as well as winter will help to keep their populations near the garden.

> **Toads eat many insects and will remain in the garden if there is water at ground level, along with hiding places.**

Snakes consume a large number of insects and some rodents. Dangerous snakes are rare and, unfortunately, so are the beneficial ones. Protect the beneficials near the garden by offering hiding places such as brush piles or boards.

Don't forget the lizards and salamanders. These skittering critters eat vast numbers of insects and are never harmful.

How about cats and dogs? In general, they are friends of the gardener because they repel wildlife pests by their very presence or as hunters. (Deer will usually avoid a garden that's energetically patrolled by a good-sized dog.) If allowed to dig in the containers under the trellis, however, cats could be a nuisance. If you apply a generous amount of powdered cayenne pepper to the soil surface, they will quickly learn to give those containers a wide berth.

So we've discussed the good guys and the bad guys when it comes to the flying, creepy-crawly, and other creatures that may

Figure 9.8. A bird bath in your garden keeps the pest patrol "staff" handy and happy.   FOREST STARR & KIM STARR/ WIKIMEDIA COMMONS

visit your garden. There are some pretty powerful arguments for tolerating a great number of insects in the garden—the neutral or beneficial as well as the "pests." They are all part of the overall balance. It's the old food-chain trick: The pests are food that maintain the population of beneficial predators.

Weed and pest control is clearly a matter of personal choice. You'll need to make a conscious decision prior to starting any pest management program—in fact, before starting a garden. Some questions to consider: Are my plants worth erecting barriers and winter protection, patrolling, or perhaps employing deliberate pest management techniques? What amount of damage (such as insect-chewed leaves or wildlife invasion) am I willing to live with? Your threshold, standards, and the purpose of your garden are all highly individual matters. If these kinds of questions are asked and answered in advance, many of the remaining pest management choices fall easily into place.

Should you find yourself facing a pest problem that has you confused or frustrated, try checking out your state's extension service website or office for help and answers.

10 Recognizing Plant Diseases and Problems

SINCE IT WOULD TAKE a large volume (or two or three) to completely cover plant diseases, I haven't attempted to include everything in here. Instead I will address the basic and most frequently occurring maladies, including recognition of the most common diseases and what to do about them. You can find much more information about plant diseases at your local library, extension service office, or at reputable online sites.

What are the symptoms that a plant is in trouble? A white coating on your squash leaves, for instance, would likely indicate a powdery mildew infection. Holes in leaves or other indications of chewing by insects are a sign of trouble, too. Finding your tomatoes rotting on the bottom—erk! Before we get into specifics for each plant, let's look at what causes the problems.

Diseases and Their Causes

We'll check out diseases first. Simply put, pathogens are the main culprits: They are living organisms that can incite a disease, which can then spread from an infected plant to a healthy plant. Kind of gives you the creeps, doesn't it? Examples of these pathogens are bacteria, fungi, viruses, nematodes, and parasitic plants. While some pathogens are restricted to a single plant species, others can infect a single plant genus, and still others attack a large number of hosts spanning many plant genera. Noninfectious (or nonliving) factors can also cause some plant diseases. These include problems we associate with growing conditions, such as drought and freezing damage, nutrient imbalances, and damage from air pollution.

Unless you grow all of your plants yourself . . . you could bring an infection into your garden.

Any part of a pathogen that can cause infection is called inoculum. Examples of this would be fungal spores, bacterial cells, nematode eggs, or virus particles. If inoculum survives the winter and causes the original or primary infection during the following spring, it is referred to as primary inoculum. Additional infections throughout the growing season can be caused by secondary inoculum.

This may sound awfully complex and nerdy, yet it's important for you to know. Unless you grow all of your plants yourself, in sterile pots and in sterile growing medium, you could bring an infection into your garden. Garden centers and other commercial plant sources, as well as friends and fellow gardeners, could have any of these diseases in their soils or plants. So when you transplant from their container to yours, the disease would come along for the ride.

If you know the enemy, you'll know what to look for. The entire crop of a plant—or range of plants—that you're trying so hard to bring to harvest can be compromised at least and decimated at worst by inoculum. It can be disseminated passively by rain, wind, insect vectors, tools, and humans. It can spread actively as nematodes or fungal zoospores swimming through water.

Now don't panic! Only a fraction of inoculum ever lands on a susceptible host. Most typically land on material that can't be infected. A tremendous surplus of inoculum is produced by most pathogens, though, which is why we gardeners must remain watchful of the signs that some unseen invader is lurking among our plants.

Fungi

Fungi are one of the most common pathogens. Around 100,000 fungal species have been identified; most are beneficial or benign. There are actually only about 8,000 fungal species that cause plant diseases. (*Only,* she says? Well, compare that amount to 100,000!) Think about what plants need in order to thrive, the stuff that makes them green, called chlorophyll. Yep, that's the same stuff you learned in science class. Fungi lack chlorophyll; they can't manufacture their own food. They need other living things for their sustenance, and so they prey on our plants.

A spore is the main reproductive unit of a fungus. The structure of these is how we can differentiate and identify the various fungi. Let's look at some common fungi that turn up in our gardens.

Three very common fungi are the water molds, downy mildews, and white rust. The water molds are dependent on wet conditions for reproduction and growth. Their spores can survive adverse conditions, and they produce motile spores capable of swimming through water.

Two important genera of these are *Pythium* and *Phytophthora. Pythium* causes diseases such as damping off as well as seed decay and root rots. (It also causes blights on turf grass.) *Phytophthora*—well, this one is famous for the disease called late

Figure 10.1. Late blight on tomatoes is not a pretty sight. Get rid of it immediately! MARY ANN HANSEN, VIRGINIA POLYTECHNIC INSTITUTE AND STATE UNIVERSITY, UNITED STATES/ WIKIMEDIA COMMONS

blight of potato that caused the great potato famine in Ireland back in 1845. And, of course, tomato early or late blight is the culprit that wipes out so many tomato crops each year; it varies from region to region as to when and how severely it occurs. *Phytophthora* (try saying that real fast 10 times!) is also the cause of root diseases on a wide variety of landscape plants, including rhododendron.

The downy mildew fungi causes diseases such as downy mildew of grape, lettuce, and onion. White rust fungus causes diseases on crucifers; its spores are dispersed by the wind.

I referred earlier to one of the most maddening problems we observe with seeds, seedlings, and seedling roots during plant propagation. It's called damping off and is caused by *Pythium*. This also affects young transplants, but it rarely kills older plants. However, these plants can develop root lesions and become stunted. Early indicators of seed rot are usually poor stands or low germination rates. Seeds become soft and mushy, then turn brown. Eventually, they simply disintegrate.

Doomed seedlings that have already popped up (emerged) suffer root damage, usually at or just below the soil line. Discoloration occurs, and the lower part of the stem becomes much thinner than the upper part of the seedling. So the seedling falls over, quickly withers, and dies. Sometimes the fungus can be seen as a fine webbing on the invaded plant tissue. There are several other fungi belonging to other fungal groups that can also cause damping off.

Bread molds have several members in their class, Zylgomycetes. (This fungus can be seen frequently on moldy bread; its spores are windblown.) An example of diseases caused by these molds it soft rot of squash. This fungal growth appears first on the blossoms or at the blossom end of the fruit. It looks like dark-headed pins in a pin cushion. Affected flowers collapse quickly; the disease spreads into the fruit, which becomes soft and begins rotting within a day or two. Inoculum of this fungi can be spread by cucumber beetles, bees, and wind. Periods of high humidity and rainfall assist this disease in its manifestation on your plants.

This is exactly why I advocate for trellising all of the cucurbit plants—squash, cucumbers, pumpkins, melons, etc. They all fare much better when their leaves and vines are up off the ground. When water, whether deliberately provided by you or dropped in rainfall, can quickly cascade off and run down the leaves and other plant parts, it helps prevent molds from getting a toehold and creating problems.

Verticillium wilt needs prominent mention here; it attacks tomatoes and potatoes. If you are gardening in containers and a raised bed, and are using uncontaminated soil, you aren't likely to be hit with this. But there are two different soilborne fungi causing this disease, and they have a very broad host range. Not only do they infect tomatoes and potatoes, they also can infect cucumber, peppers, rhubarbs, watermelons, eggplants, artichokes, broad beans, raspberries, strawberries, and a number of

Figure 10.2. Pole beans wind upward on the trellis.   GREG ASPINALL

weedy as well as woody plants. This potential problem is, then, another very good reason for getting plants up off the ground!

If you have any of the aforementioned plants growing directly in the ground, watch for wilting, the most characteristic symptom of infection by a verticillium fungus. Mid-August is when symptoms usually appear on the lower leaves of plants; infected plants wilt during the warmest part of the day and then recover at night. The leaf edges and areas between the veins will turn yellow, and then brown. Infected plants also have a V-shaped lesion at the edge of the leaf in a fan pattern. When these foliar lesions enlarge, the result is complete browning and death of the leaves.

This fungus is, in fact, the reason why I switched from growing vegetables in the ground to planting them all in containers—and turned it into an often-overlooked gardening innovation I now share with others. Here's what happened: I had nearly 60 tomato plants in the ground that year, more than half of which had succumbed to verticillium wilt. Once that fungus is in the soil, it will stay there for many years. Potatoes, tomatoes, and eggplant are three of the plants that cannot be grown in that soil again. Some agricultural authorities state that the infection period lasts a lifetime, if you are unfortunate enough to be afflicted by this fungus. Other say that a minimum of two to four years is common, and that fumigation can speed up the soil revitalization process.

When I found that this had happened to my tomatoes, at the start of the subsequent growing season I first laid out a long strip of Typar weed barrier over that diseased soil. Then I set out my tomato plants, each in its own 5-gallon container (with drain holes). Finally, I set up micro-drip irrigation for that area of the garden. And that was the end of the problem. The fungus could not go through the Typar to contaminate the plants, they received just the right amount of water, and I had a bumper crop of healthy tomatoes!

Figure 10.3. Check out 65 tomato plants, all in containers.   GREG ASPINALL

Figure 10.4. Verticillium wilt isn't something you want to see on
strawberry plants.   BRIAN PRECHTEL/ WIKIMEDIA COMMONS

Some symptoms of verticillium wilt are similar to another fungus, fusarium. However, streaking caused by it progresses farther up the stem. Infected potato tubers often show similar vascular discoloration. This occurs in rings, especially near the stem end; however, the tubers are still safe to eat, even if they are discolored in this manner.

If you want to learn more about these two fungi, I recommend that you try an online search for "verticillium wilt," and it should take you to a selection of reputable, university-based websites that will have reliable, detailed information on these and other plant diseases.

Note: There are many other fungi that affect various fruits, trees, etc. However, I have only mentioned those that commonly occur in vegetable plants.

Bacteria

Let's look briefly at bacteria, another disease-causing culprit. Galls, fire blight, and bacterial wilt can cause problems in various plants. The bacterial wilt of cucurbits is caused by a pathogen that overwinters in the gut of the cucumber beetle. The cycle of this disease begins when beetles feed on seedlings and then release bacteria into the plant's vascular system. More disease spread happens when beetles pick up bacteria from newly infected plants and then fly to healthy plants within the crop. The symptoms of wilt appear first on individual leaves, then lateral shoots, and finally the entire plant. The larger the plant is at the time of infection, the longer it will be before the first symptoms and plant death. New shoots will wilt and die back quickly. So keep an eye on the leaves of those cucurbit plants!

Parasites

Now what about those confounded nematodes? Those plant parasitic nematodes are actually tiny, microscopic worms. Many other free-living or nonplant-feeding nematode species can be found in every kind of habitat. All of these critters have a needle-like structure called a stylet. It is used like a straw to puncture plant cells; the nematode can then consume the cellular contents.

There are two classification of nematodes: Endoparasites burrow into tissues and feed internally within a plant, while ectoparasites feed from the surface of plant tissue. They can be either migratory or sedentary. The migratory types are mobile throughout all their life stages except the egg state, while sedentary forms become large and then are immobile once they start feeding.

What do they do? Soil nematodes cause damage to root tissues and interfere with the uptake of water and nutrients, from the root to the shoot. Sometimes they inject toxic substances into the cells on which they feed, causing further cell damage. Viruses can be spread by some plant parasitic nematodes. Others cause such severe feeding wounds with their stylets that other soil pathogens such as fungi and bacteria can then gain entry into damaged plants.

Some nematodes attack very specific plants; others have broad host ranges. Some can also survive and complete their life cycles on weeds. Most can survive for longer periods of time without a host, for as long as a year, due to large food reserves. Many survive the winter in frozen soil, and a few parasitic nematodes can even lie in a dormant state within a cyst for many years.

Root-knot nematodes are common and easily recognized. The northern root-knot nematode creates small galls on strawberries and many ornamental plants. Tomatoes, cucurbits, and carrots can fall victim to the southern root-knot nematode, which causes large root galls on the plants.

The lesion nematode is another that's commonly encountered. They are endoparasites of plant roots and burrow through the root cortex. Plants with many dead roots and roots with brown lesions are indicators of their presence. Plants typically attacked by lesion nematodes include many tomatoes, strawberries, annual and perennial ornamentals, and many turf grass cultivars.

Ever hear of parasitic *plants?* There are several seed plants that are capable of parasitizing other plants. Broomrape, witchweed, dodder, and mistletoe are some examples. The last two attach themselves to aerial portions of a plant; the first two attach to plant roots. In some states, these plants won't show up. But dodder, which is the only parasitic plant common in home gardens in New York State, does latch onto other plants. It produces twining yellow to orange stems resembling spaghetti and also produces small structures that actually penetrate into the host plant's vascular system. All nourishment for the dodder plant is derived directly from the host plant.

Viruses

We're almost done with the diseases, but we can't forget to take a look at plant viruses. Boy, are they a pain! They differ from all other plant pathogens because they're not made up of cells and can only be seen with the help of an electron microscope. Viruses don't divide, nor do they produce any kind of reproductive structures such as spores. They multiply by taking control of the plant, forcing it to manufacture *more* virus particles. Viruses not only spread within infected plant tissues, they can also be spread to other plants by vectors such as insects and nematodes.

Serological tests and genetic sequencing are currently the most common methods used to detect viruses. Most plant viruses cause systemic infections. Unfortunately, once a plant is infected with a virus, it's infected for life; there is no cure. Cells aren't killed by the virus consuming them, but instead the normal cellular processes of the plant are disrupted.

Insects, mites, nematodes, fungi, and parasitic plants are the vectors relied upon by viruses in nature. They can also be spread by pollen, sap, seeds, and vegetative propagation. That's why infected plants must immediately be isolated, removed, and destroyed, before nearby healthy plants are infected. One saving grace of viruses is that they require living cells to multiply.

Some of the most maddening viruses common to vegetable gardens is the tomato spotted wilt virus. It has a very wide host range, including many commonly grown ornamental flowers, vegetables, and common weeds.

Environment-Caused Maladies

Thank goodness that disorders caused by environmental factors aren't contagious, even though they can cause substantial plant damage. We've all seen the effects of droughts, hurricanes, flooding, severe thunderstorms, blizzards, deep freezes, etc. These are things that we can do nothing to prevent and little to abate, but we can try, huh? Do pay attention to local weather forecasts and seasonal predictions made by the weather service and farmer's almanacs. They can be very, very helpful.

Table 10.1. Plant diseases and symptoms

Diseases	Symptoms	Susceptible plants
Bacterial diseases	Galls, blights, rots, leaf spots	Corn, cucumber, tomato, cherry, plum
Black leg	Darkening at base of plant	Cabbage, cauliflower
Blights	General killing of leaves, flowers, stems	Tomato
Club root	Distorted swollen roots	Cabbage, cauliflower, broccoli
Damping off	Sudden wilting of seedlings or rotting of roots in soil	Seedlings in general
Dodder	Parasitic seed plant with orange tendrils	Ornamentals and vegetables in general
Downy mildew	White, gray, or violet patches	Grape, lettuce, onion
Galls	Noticeable enlargements of leaves, stems, or roots	Tomato
Nematodes	Cause decline diseases	Tomato, strawberry
Nonparasitic diseases	Due to environmental conditions rather than specific organisms	Plants in general
Powdery mildew	Superficial white powdery growth on leaves and flowers	Apple, grape, cucumber, squash
Rots	Soft or hard decay or disintegration of plant tissues	Apple, peach, grape, tomato, potato, squash
Scurf	Flaky or scaly lesions	Potato
Smuts	Sooty black spore masses	Corn
Viral diseases	Mosaics, ring spot, yellows, wilt caused by viruses	Fruits and vegetables, and ornamentals in general

Growth reduction in plants can result from lower-than-optimum levels of nutrients. Chronic nutrient deficiency can result in severe decline—even death, in extreme situations. If certain minerals or salts are present in high concentrations, they can interfere with normal plant metabolism. A common problem seen in home gardens is blossom end rot of tomatoes; it's caused by a localized calcium deficiency in the fruits. Water stress can bring it on, and excessive amounts of fertilizer also help to reduce the uptake of calcium from the soil. So you must avoid overfertilization of your tomato plants and keep moisture levels constant and consistent to help prevent the development of blossom end rot.

Another common symptom of problems in a plant is yellowing leaves, or chlorosis. This can be caused by a deficiency of iron, zinc, or manganese, or induced by the careless disposal of waste materials. This is why I speak so strongly against the use of fill dirt in any kind of garden!

Diagnosis

So how do you figure out which of these and other maladies has struck your plants should you find some of them looking just plain sick? To conclude this chapter, table 10.1 provides names of plant diseases, symptoms, and examples of susceptible plants. It will give you a foundation to start with should you find signs of disease or damage on your plants.

Meanwhile, be vigilant so that you can head off plant problems before they get the upper hand. Try to faithfully inspect your garden plant by plant at least once a week—more, if time allows. Pay particular attention during and after extended hot, dry weather and also if extremely wet weather persists.

Well, that's it for this chapter. You should now have a basic foundation to help you recognize—and even head off—plant disease problems in your garden. May all your plants be healthy ones.

11 Good Ideas from Other People

NOW YOU CAN RELAX; this is a mostly pictorial (and very short) chapter showing what some other people built after seeing my off-the-ground garden. They are all what I consider good ideas and show how much variation there is in doing off-the-ground gardening. As I said earlier, the methods and structures I've described in this book are concepts and suggested techniques that can be tweaked and still be successful.

We'll start off with a unique take on the straw-based raised beds. In fact, this is what I call a "four-poster raised bed." Take a close look at figure 11.1, and you'll see why.

This creation was built by the folks at a nearby assisted-living center, after the staff and several residents saw my presentation about off-the-ground gardening methods. The raised bed was to serve a twofold purpose. First, their chef desired a kitchen garden to use in cooking healthy meals for the residents. The raised bed would make a perfect, low-maintenance, easily accessed growing spot for herbs and other small plants. Second, the center's activity

Figure 11.1. This is the famous four-poster raised bed, about half-full of straw.

Figure 11.2. Here's everything needed for a healthy meal—delicious!

GREG ASPINALL

coordinator wanted a place for their ambulatory residents to go out into the fresh air and dig their fingers into the soil. Those who used canes, walkers, and even wheelchairs were able to do this once the raised-bed garden was set up, and they had a ball making their way outside and watching the plants grow like mad.

Figure 11.3. Ninety-three-year-old Agnes Dickens gets around the garden just fine.   GREG ASPINALL

Some even assisted in planting the seeds. (I did have to laugh, though. One woman, a former master gardener herself, was very skeptical at first, saying my techniques would "never work." She ended up literally eating her words and enjoyed all of the edibles immensely!) Both purposes were served beautifully, and the residents greatly enjoyed the resulting salad bars and herb-enhanced entrées at their meals.

As you can see in figure 11.4, they chose to use solid, wide boards for the sides at the top, then added the chicken wire for the lower part of the sides. Instead of squaring off the corners with a box frame, they used strong cedar posts at the corners. I thought it was a great idea, and it worked just fine. The hanging pots were a cute touch and added a touch of whimsy.

Figure 11.4. The four-poster raised bed, full of growing plants with more in pots hanging on the corners.

Figure 11.5. The Carlson's first raised bed, with sprayers turned on. Can you see the turkey wire used on the sides?

We also helped them put up a trellis, and they rounded up various containers and bought a few of the black dishpans to use, too. The center had a very successful year with their garden, and the very pleased owners allowed for growth and enhancement of the area in the following year (2011). I am happy to report that it, too, was a resounding success.

Next, let's take a look at the Carlsons' garden. (You may have noticed their name in the acknowledgments in the front of this book.) After visiting my garden on a countywide garden tour in 2010, they hurried home and started putting together the components. Since Dud is a retired shop teacher, he had all kinds of fun building—and improving on—the structures he'd seen.

For instance, for his raised bed he chose to use turkey wire rather than chicken wire or hardware cloth—great idea! (See fig. 11.5.) He also scrounged locally for food-grade 5-gallon buckets

Figure 11.6. Talk about production gardening—here are the 5-gallon buckets all laid out.

Figure 11.7. Each bucket has its own dripper ready to keep the plants happily watered.

and put his large plants into them, setting up a micro-drip irrigation for them, too. (See fig. 11.6 and fig. 11.7.) The latter concept
was new to him, and he was astounded at its simplicity and effi-
ciency, along with the savings in water volume. Then he found a
free ornamental patio arbor frame and set that up for trellising
plants. It's both attractive and functional. (See fig. 11.8.) Dud also
found the wonderful, heavy-duty commercial weed barrier mentioned in chapter 2 and covered the ground with it prior to placing
his structures and containers on it.

Figure 11.8. This ornamental arbor was scrounged from someone's
discards; it serves as the framework for a trellising system.

Figure 11.9. What a lovely sight—raised bed and containers all sitting on weed barrier. Talk about weed-free gardening!

When Dud and Nan came by my garden again for the 2011 countywide garden tour, they couldn't wait to share their photographs with me. Was I amazed! When I saw what they had done, I couldn't have been more pleased; they had taken my ideas and improved on them immensely. (See fig. 11.9 for a look at their setup in action.) They learned something new, and so did I.

Finally, a local fruit orchardist whose property is adjacent to ours saw my methods, and the wheels started turning in his head. He got the idea of making what is essentially a structure similar to the concrete-block composting bin. (See fig. 11.10 and fig. 11.11.) However, he filled it with a soilless mixture and started

Figure 11.10. These plants are all bushing out from a soilless mixture, easlly managed in these concrete and PVC-pipe beds.

Figure 11.11. A bumper crop of tomatoes and other plants gratifies this garden's owner, year after year.

plants from seed in it. What a terrific idea—you should have seen his tomatoes and other goodies, which grew like wildfire in that off-the-ground bed!

I know that there are other people around here who've also built variations on the straw-based raised bed; I just wasn't able to get photographs of them. But you can see that there's plenty of room for creativity and innovation, including very thrifty ways of doing this off-the-ground gardening. Just be sure to always keep the basics in mind: good drainage, good direct sunlight, and keeping plants healthy. I'm sure that if you follow those simple precepts, you'll have great success in your new way of gardening.

Index